Lord of the Valleys

behold it is I . . . that saith unto Zion,
THY GOD REIGNETH!

ISAIAH 52:6–7

Lord of the Valleys

FLORENCE BULLE

LOGOS INTERNATIONAL

Plainfield, New Jersey

1972

All Scriptures are from the King James Version of the Bible unless otherwise identified in the footnotes.

INTERNATIONAL STANDARD BOOK NUMBER: 912106-01-8
LIBRARY OF CONGRESS CATALOG CARD NUMBER: 72-85630
© 1972 LOGOS, INTERNATIONAL, PLAINFIELD, N.J. 07060
PRINTED IN THE UNITED STATES OF AMERICA
BY THE COLONIAL PRESS INC., CLINTON, MASSACHUSETTS

with love
to Al

and

to the SHEPHERD KING—
    the KING of KINGS
and to all
    the shepherds
        He sent
            to show me the way.

Contents

Preface ix

Introduction xv

1. I Walk through This Valley 1

2. Lord of the Valleys 15

3. Why the Valleys? 27

4. Learning a Servant's Role—in the Valley 43

5. Learning Love—in the Valley 58

6. Understanding the Goodness of God 73

7. Who Builds the Fences? 81

8. I Cannot Choose 91

9. He Maketh Me to Rest—in the Valley 98

10. Alone with God—in the Valley 105

11. Weakness Becomes an Asset 114

12. Being Understood or Understanding Him 121

13. Getting Rid of the Hang-ups 132

14. Panic Praying 144

15. Faith That Stands Still—in the Valley 158

16. Bringing Us into Balance 165

17. Healing?—in the Valley 172

18. The Ministry of Suffering—in the Valley 188

19. Rejoicing in Hope—Triumphant in the Valley 195

Notes 203

Preface

I think what caused me to see her apart from the other passengers was that she was so obviously at ease with herself. Quite taken up with the paperback she was reading, she sat directly across the aisle, trim and attractive in a navy blue dress edged in white, her face lightly sprinkled with freckles, and should sunlight have touched her short, curly blonde hair, I am sure it would have seemed gilded.

There was the lurid voice of a woman, loud and encroaching from the front of the bus; the girl's head came up. Whether her eyes were gray or green behind smoky blue frames, I don't remember. But they were smiling, and her comment, witty and affable, invited conversation.

I certainly wouldn't have guessed that she was a "teaching-Sister" in a parochial school. When she told me she had graduated from Notre Dame, I asked if she was acquainted with the charismatic prayer groups reportedly meeting on campus.

"Oh, you mean Pentecostal," she said candidly.

It is a word I rather seek to avoid because it is so easily misconstrued. But I knew what she meant and nodded.

"Oh, yes." She leaned toward me, her eyes sparkly. "Isn't it tremendous what God is doing today!"

It *is* wonderful what God is doing. And tremendously exciting. Even the very way in which the two of us, a Catholic and a Protestant, communicated that day was evidence of that something new which is happening.

Unquestionably, this is an hour in which the move of the Holy Spirit is challenging the church universal to a new dimension of faith. However, the miracles and manifestations of the Spirit which are inciting many to a fresh concept of the power of God have, unfortunately, become a religion in themselves to many zealous souls—a religion which holds with inflexible tenacity that a right relationship to God presupposes health, wealth, and access to a spiritual computer, autogenetic for solving all of life's problems.

Consequently, many who suffer affliction and adversity are floundering in confusion and despair. In the wake of extreme emphasis on the miraculous, I have seen faith shot down when God did not always heal or deliver or produce according to "the rules." And some, embittered by seeming tragedy, have turned from God and spat on the church when divine intervention was not forthcoming. All they understood was that God hadn't done what somebody told them He would do. Disillusioned, they had plummeted to total defeat.

But are physical and material blessings proof of a right relationship to God?

Is the miraculous an accurate yardstick by which to measure spiritual stature?

Is total commitment to the Lordship of Jesus Christ secured only through the manifestation of the supernatural? Or through faith and obedience in the midst of affluence, affliction, adversity, or whatever?

And what about the valleys?

As soon as physical suffering, extreme difficulties, and "impossible" situations come into the life of a Christian, the question will undoubtedly be raised: Did this man sin or did his father? In some groups, it is almost certain the devil will be rebuked, demons exorcised, and fire called down from heaven as a matter of course. Part of the grandstand will hold that it is the lot of the righteous to suffer while others will contend that suffering is the destiny of the wicked. And there are bound to be those who will simply shrug and say it is life.

Very few, however, will see divine planning and purpose in the valleys. Very few will understand that God has not been standing apart while these things were "happening," that He is not only present, but that with His own hand He has formed every valley of the soul—that He is Lord not only of the hills, but of the valleys too.

The reality of this truth and the learning that has come out of personal experience are what this book is about. In all honesty it is a book conceived and brought to birth in deep valleys.

If your faith has been shattered by tragedy or shaken through adversity, believe me, I understand how it is. And I pray that God will use my sharing some of the answers He gave to me, to bring you to the same personal discovery that Jesus is Lord—regardless.

Only when we see Him reigning in the valleys and choose to come under His rule, can we walk through the valleys in triumph. Even so, God would lift up your head, and have you to look and know:

"Thus saith the Lord . . . my people shall know my name
. . . that I am he that doth speak:"

F. B.
Houghton, N.Y.
1972

Acknowledgments

With heartfelt thanks—

To Judson Cornwall who carried the manuscript with him twice across this continent, three times into Canada, and once into Alaska, snatching moments from his exhausting schedule that he might give me the first critical evaluation.

To Bob Mumford for sharing Jesus in the way that he did, for his confidence in what God was doing, and for graciously consenting to write the foreword.

To W. C. Frykman, Major William Barr and Helen E. Hull for releasing articles by the author previously published in *Fellowship*, *The War Cry*, and *Light and Life Evangel*.

To Zondervan Publishing House for permission to use Scriptures taken from *The Amplified Bible, Old Testament*, © 1962, 64, by Zondervan Publishing House.

To The Lockman Foundation for permission to use Scriptures taken from *The Amplified Bible, New Testament*, © 1958 by The Lockman Foundation.

To Ministry of Life for permission to quote from Watchman Nee's *Release of the Spirit*, © 1965.

To Tyndale House Publishers for permission to use Scriptures taken from *The Living Bible*, © 1971.

To Willard and Mae, and Jeannie and Jim for the ready loan of their typewriters, when mine repeatedly went berserk.

To Irene Harrell, writer and copy editor, who so generously shared her know-how in doing the copy editing.

To my wonderful family, who, I think, would often gladly trade me off for a nonwriter.

To my mother, Myrtie Schoolcraft, to my "other mother," May Johnson, to the wonderful gals of our prayer-fellowship, along with everyone else who stood with me in prayer and faith and love during the writing. They share in the accomplishment. Even as God told me, the book has only been brought to birth as the result of "many voices turned Godward," that they too might "give thanks on our behalf for the grace granted us" (II Cor. 1:11 *Amplified Bible*).

To those who have shared with me what I have shared herein.

But most of all, to my wonderful Lord for His love and light and Life. Without Him, I can do nothing.

Introduction

When we were children, we used to play the game called "king of the mountain." The object was to remain on top while others sought to pull you down. Life has this tendency, too, attempting to pull us down from our place on the mountains.

It is of primary importance that we come to know our Lord Jesus Christ as "King of the mountain," that is, the transcendent and triumphant Jesus whom God has made both Lord and Christ. But it is equally important to see Him as Lord of the valley. Somehow, continual one-sided teaching on the glorified Christ leaves us stripped of the ministry of that One who was also touched with our infirmities.

I have known the author of this book for several years, and feel God has given her some particular ability to record and describe subjective feelings. These "feelings" are the dealings of God in her life, and have become the basis for this effective and helpful manuscript. Some books, of necessity, are written for a restricted reading audience; this book is of that nature. Though it may not speak to everyone, those for whom it is intended will find a ministry of life and light.

Due to the nature of the book, and knowledge of the complicated life situation of the author, I expected a subtle "poor me" to ooze up between the words (surely it would have been justified). Florence has delightfully managed to avoid the unavoidable and bless the Body of Christ with her word of honest testimony.

The Promised Land of spiritual progress is a land peaked with glorious spiritual experiences *and* valleys which lie between. With this author, let us move from mountain to mountain by coming to know the *Lord of the Valleys.*

—*Bob Mumford*

Lord of the Valleys

This is my valley
—a lonely place
A place of brokenness
Of learning
The shattering of *my* dreams
That I may know *His vision*
The greater glory
of Reality.

"Look at your way in the valley; know what you have done—" [1]

—*Jeremiah*

1.

I Walk through This Valley

I was a long-legged, skinny child, bony as a mountain-man's hound dog, and high-strung as a rich man's racehorse. There were too many years between myself and my classmates: kids my own age were still in grade school when I had finished junior high. I felt it keenly that I didn't "belong" with either group, and outgoing though I was, I was very lonely. At the same time, I had a deep and intense desire to know God.

Looking back, I well remember the unsatisfied hunger of my heart. I wouldn't have known how to express it except in the religious vocabulary I had grown up with and spoke fluently. But the terminology, as I understood it, didn't begin to express what I felt. So prayer was more a projection of that longing Godward than it was words.

At some time, though, so long ago I can't remember when, there was born within my spirit this prayer: "Lord Jesus, take me into the depths alone with You." And through the years it continued to be the cry of my heart. Had I known where the answer would take me, I'd probably have gone back to, "Now I lay me down to sleep . . ."

As to the way God was to answer, I cannot point to any precise

1

moment and say this is where it all began. But I think I know when the awareness that God was beginning "something new," began to seep into my spiritual consciousness.

It was October, 1955. The San Francisco Bay fog had rolled quietly up the valley during the night, tucking its blanket securely around our town, shrouding it completely in damp folds. Its penetrating chill seemed to seep through the house, and no matter how high I turned the thermostat, I still shivered.

I would have preferred to stay indoors on such a day, but I had an appointment to keep, so there was nothing to do but turn my coat collar up a little higher and step out into the cold gray mist.

I drove slowly because of the fog. It was a short trip to the doctor's office, and I was soon opening the door marked *Chest Clinic: Diseases of the Heart and Lungs.* I couldn't have counted the number of times I had read those words in the past two years.

"Hi, Florence!" the doctor's pretty receptionist greeted me. We had become fast friends during my many visits. "Come on in! Doctor will be with you in a minute." She showed me into one of the doctor's private offices.

We chatted a moment before she returned to her work. The door swung shut behind her and I was left alone.

I sat there looking at the pale yellow walls, the diplomas and class pictures, the large photographs of the doctor's three children and the small one of his father—I knew them all so well.

I remembered the first time I had met Dr. T., two years earlier. I had been rushed to the hospital after a severe lung hemorrhage, and he had been summoned by the hospital's chief of staff.

After introducing himself, he had checked my condition. From my charts and previous record, he knew what the trouble was. He turned to me abruptly.

"You're going to have to have radical chest surgery," he said.

"Oh, no, I'm not!" I was just as adamant as he was positive.

"You have bronchiectasis in such an advanced stage that you're having violent hemorrhages—in both lungs." He shook his head.

"At best, your life span will be halved. You're twenty-eight years old now. Do you know what that means?"

Quickly I did some mental arithmetic. I didn't like the answer I came up with.

In 1941, twelve years before my first meeting with Dr. T., I had suffered a slight hemorrhage. From then on they had become more frequent and more severe. Finally a chest specialist told us that the disease had advanced too far for surgery. But new techniques in surgery had been developed, and now Dr. T. felt it was the only chance I had.

I pointed to the picture of my children on my bedside stand. I couldn't keep the tears back. I choked on the words: "I'm ready to go—I'm not afraid for myself. But my boys—they're so little . . ."

The doctor's smile was full of compassion as he said softly, "That's why I'm here to help you, so you'll be able to raise them."

"We've had nothing but doctor and hospital bills, ever since we've been married." I was sobbing now.

"There are very few people who could afford the type of surgery or the care that you are going to need, but it's not going to cost you a penny—and you'll get the best we know how to give you."

I could scarcely believe my ears. I knew that Dr. T. was one of the outstanding chest surgeons in the West. He had left, making an appointment to discuss the whole matter with my husband that same evening.

Carefully and in detail, he explained the procedure to us both. He would remove the diseased portion of one lung now. A year later, a similar operation would be made on the other lung.

"You'll have rough going for a year or two," he concluded, "but then all this trouble will be in the past."

"Will I be able to play tennis and swim again?" I asked eagerly.

"I'm sure you will," he said confidently.

Then I wept uncontrollable tears of joy—because of the hope of getting well.

But that hope would be shattered again and again. First the

shock of sinus surgery, performed to reduce the chance of later infection, brought on bronchospastic asthma. Then, two months after the first segmental resection of one lung, complications developed which could not be relieved by a tube inserted under local anesthesia, and I was back in surgery for five more hours.

Eight months later, it seemed imperative to proceed with surgery on the other lung at once. This time there was a lobectomy as well as a resection. After two weeks I went home, but eight hours later my only good remaining lobe ruptured. The pain was so severe that when I arrived at the hospital every bit of my clothing was soaking wet with perspiration—the nurses could wring water out of it. Again a tube had to be inserted with only a local anesthetic, and I felt as though my nerves were almost at the breaking point.

A few months later I was back in the hospital hemorrhaging again. It happened several times that year.

And now I was facing another crisis.

The jangling telephone brought me back to the little room with the pale yellow walls. The door opened and the doctor's jovial grin greeted me. He winked and settled himself at his desk, where he took the call.

The receiver clicked as he replaced it on the hook. And then he was leaning forward across the desk, and we were chatting and laughing about the latest antics of our youngsters. They never failed to provide plenty of material for conversation.

There was a pause as Dr. T. went over to the X-ray case and switched on the light. Withdrawing the X rays from their big brown envelope, he slipped them into place. I had had a bronchogram a couple of days earlier, and these were the pictures.

There had been some evidence of new trouble, and so perhaps I was somewhat prepared for the doctor's verdict—but a strange inner resistance sometimes causes one to continue to hope when faced with insurmountable odds and prevents one's ever being really ready to accept unwelcome facts.

"I'm sorry, Florence. You have a new spread in the lower right lobe . . ."

All the past, present, and future were squished together into a minute particle of time. I was in the center, with the doctor's words beating against my mind.

I smiled—from habit, I suppose. I could see the hurt in his eyes. I knew how hard he had tried, the tedious hours of surgery, the midnight hours he had kept vigil beside my bed, the meals he had left uneaten because I needed emergency care, the time he had spent fighting for my life. My chest surgeon had been more than my doctor, he had been a real friend. My whole family had learned to know and to love him. I was determined he would not know how disappointed I was—he had tried so desperately hard.

I believe my concern for his disappointment helped to cushion the initial shock. But then, as the impact of his words began to penetrate my mind, and as I began to realize their full implication, I had a strange sense of numbness.

"The Lord is my light and my salvation; whom shall I fear? The Lord is the strength of my life; of whom shall I be afraid." [2] I had walked through the valley of the shadow time and again with those words on my lips and with their assurance in my heart. Now they were wrung from my heart—not in faith, but in desperation—and I silently repeated them over and over.

"Where do we go from here?" I managed a weak smile.

Dr. T. met my gaze squarely. "I don't know. Perhaps we may be forced to do more surgery. Perhaps a dry desert climate would stop the condition from spreading farther. I just don't know all the answers. I don't think anyone does."

I have always appreciated Dr. T.'s frankness, and I was able to discuss the facts calmly. I therefore knew what I must learn to accept—unless God did a miracle.

When I left his office, he saw me to the door. I said good-bye, and stepped out into the chill fall air.

I seemed to move automatically. I slipped behind the wheel of my car, but I didn't turn on the ignition.

How long I sat there, I do not know. But suddenly, I was aware of the Lord's presence. I felt no terrific surge of faith, no intense emotional upsweep. I saw no vision, I heard no voice. But He was there.

"The Lord is my light and my salvation: whom shall I fear? The Lord is the strength of my life; of whom shall I be afraid?" I whispered the words in faith this time, for His strength had become mine.

And then I was aware that the fog had completely lifted. The bright sunlight bathed the town in its warmth. Everything was the same—nothing had changed—but the scope of my vision had been diminished because of the fog. Now once again I could see clearly. God had not changed—I had only been unable to see Him clearly when, for a passing moment, He had been obscured by my unworthy fears.

My new knowledge of my own condition changed nothing. If God was the same, I could continue to walk confidently into the future, serene in the knowledge that I was in His hands, that His mercies are new every morning. In His strength, I could face each new day as it came.

I started the car and headed for home.[3]

Shortly thereafter, we did move, following what we thought were the doctor's orders. But we soon found the orders came from higher up: God was moving to answer the prayer that I had long been praying; it was the beginning of that "something new" He would do.

Unknown to us at the time, nine hundred miles away, a pastor had built a church as God moved him to share his discovery of "the victorious life." He had prayed specifically that God would send in those who were searching for deeper truths. It was here God led us through those circumstances which seemed so difficult at the time. Under the anointed ministry of this pastor, I made a discovery which would change the whole course of my life: one does not become spiritual by osmosis: it has to come from within. And I began to understand how chronic exposure had left me surfeited with religion, but with a terrible want of spiritual life.

As a child, I lived on the main highway running north and south from California to Canada. Since we had several spare bedrooms and Dad and Mother always made preachers welcome, our home was sort of a preacher's hotel, nonprofit. Whenever there were special meetings, we usually kept the evangelist.

Many ministers who stayed in our home were prominent personalities in their respective denominations. Most were real friends, grandpas and uncles to me. Exposure to men of this caliber enriched my life, as well as adding sparkle.

I've heard sanctification argued till long after midnight: suppression vs. eradication. My main conclusion was that the suppressionists weren't very suppressed, and the eradicationists weren't very eradicated. My parents agreed with neither theory, nor entirely with each other. This added even more zest to the discussions. Similarly, the pros and cons of eternal security were argued so vehemently at times that I was convinced both sides would stand a much better chance of getting into heaven by switching their viewpoint.

My parents were very strict and rigidly opinionated. Even so, Mother's reaction to the Pentecostals was quite apart from the majority who considered them way-out. Such judging, generally completely unknowledgeable, fired Mother to back more than one of their critics into a corner. I can still see the glint in her eyes as she would say, "The Bible plainly states that *some* will speak with tongues. What I want to know—where are the *some* in our church?

Semiprivately, Mother thought the tone of the Pentecostals' services too loud, the tempo too fast, and the time too long—but she knew her Bible. And she was a born debater.

As a family, we joined a couple of different Holiness churches when I was a child. Dad at one time or other spoke in most of the

churches in our city. On rare occasions we visited the large Pentecostal assembly where some of our friends were members. My closest girl friend was Catholic. And the community church Dad later
pastored represented eighteen different denominations. So when
anyone asks my denominational background, I'm inclined to reply,
"mongrel."

In fact, I can scarcely think of a denomination which has not in
some way touched our lives and left us the richer. All of these asso-
ciations have made me to know the reality of the Body of Christ
being made up of all believers everywhere who love and serve the
Lord Jesus Christ.

But in spite of this wide exposure to the ministry of various
groups, no one ever got through to me with the answer to my need.
I recognized that many knew God in a real way. But even today,
certain names bring to mind some eccentric behavior, fanatical
quirk, affected mannerism, a one-string doctrine, an exposé, or self-
ordained style of ministry. Each seemed to think he needed a peculiar identity to achieve recognition or status. The pity was that
not one left me with a practical answer to what, even then, I was
searching for.

I didn't find it in the church, either. Depending on the group,
seven or eight "don'ts" in the little black church Discipline judged
you a Christian. I suppose there were a few "dos" too. But mostly I
remember the "don'ts," and the stereotyped testimony, "I'm glad
I'm saved and sanctified . . . and I'm going all the way with Him."

I was never quite sure what was meant by "all the way with
Him," since often the persons testifying weren't even on speaking
terms with some of the other members. And heaven forbid they
should be seen in the company of publicans, harlots, and sinners!

All the way with Him? Well, I suppose they could sit on the
porch steps while He went inside to dinner.

Once, I tried to express the deep longing within me for more of
God to a minister high up in evangelical ecclesiastical circles. Pat-
ting me on the shoulder, he said, "My dear, with an honest face like

yours—you don't have a thing to worry about." It would have been funny if it wasn't so tragic.

Strangely, the more I saw and heard, the more convinced I became that if life was to have any real meaning this side of eternity, there must be horizons in God which went far beyond narrow bigoted, introverted, "Bless-me clubs." Something within cried out to explore, to discover that which I sensed should mark the church as the body of the Living Christ. Saturated with religion, I groped for reality and life.

It would take a lot of unlearning, and a long way of being led through interminable valleys of darkness and despair before God would begin to turn my captivity.

Though God had begun doing something new in our lives through our move to Tucson, Arizona, and we were being grounded in the "applied" Word, still Jesus as Lord meant little more to me than the expression of His title.

Then in another strategic move, I found myself again being uprooted and settled into a completely new and extremely difficult situation. Here for the first time I was confronted with the Lordship of Jesus Christ as it related to me personally.

Finally it began to get through. Life was no game to be played where the "pieces" that interlock to make up the whole could be separated and counted off: "One for You, Lord . . . one for me . . . one for You, Lord . . . one for me . . ."

I was brought face to face with the fact that the claims of His Lordship were, without any reservation, to my whole life—to every second of every twenty-four hours of my time, and that they pertained to my every action, reaction, and attitude. His authority was absolute; my submission must be also.

This was not something to be lived in a super-spiritual realm. It applied very practically to my daily duties as wife and mother, spreading out to include all other relationships and situations. If Jesus was to be absolute Lord of my life—His legitimate position—that all included an "awe-full" lot!

Lacking so much in understanding, I was frightened as I contemplated what complete acquiescence to the all-inclusiveness of Christ's claims might mean. What understanding I did have, made me just as scared to reject them. Fear became an obsession, unreasonable, incomprehensible.

My frantic, stubborn determination to retain at least a checkrein on my behavior and future course precipitated a violent clashing of my will with the supreme claim of Jesus Christ, as Lord, to absolute control. I argued that the principle of "total submission" was impossible, insipid, unfair, preposterous. Why, I would become nothing more than a vegetable! I didn't care to become a carrot to be chewed or a potato to be mashed at another person's will—without even a reactive groan.

Ridiculous? Of course! But "being a vegetable" was my analogy for "total submission."

I held that since God had created me a free, moral, thinking individual, it was only reasonable to assume that I had certain "rights," at least the right to a voice and some self-assertion. But my contorted mental gymnastics got me nowhere. They only landed me in a broken heap. Then, in His mercy, God gave me a tremendous revelation of His love. From that point, I knew, and would always know, that His unqualified claim to all of my life came out of the deepest expression of that love.

There are so many determining influences over which we cannot possibly have any control; we only kid ourselves if we think to be our own masters. Recognizing this as true, however, only leaves us more insecure than ever unless we discover the One who holds all things in His hands, and learn that submission to Him is the only real security we can ever know.

The Lord is no tyrannical despot. Out of His unfathomable love, He was offering me the security of His control. I had nothing to fear by committing my whole self to Him who was not only love, but perfection.

In fact, this was the very act which released the divine flow of His love throughout my being, bringing about an instantaneous deliverance and transformed attitude. What I had refused to accept, I now embraced. The struggle was over.

From that moment on, fused into my conscious and subconscious was the intense desire that Jesus Christ rule every area of my life—regardless. To this end I had made a rock-bottom commitment which I have never retracted. Whatever I have faced, even when I've wrestled for my own way or struggled against the complete acceptance of His ways, God has held me faithfully to that commitment. Continually, He works out the reality of that surrender in ways which I could never have foreseen.

Eight years before this book began to take definite form, we were on vacation. I had been asked to speak at the Sunday morning service in a church with which I was only vaguely familiar. It was just a year after my commitment to the Lord.

We had been visiting back and forth between our families, staying that week with my mother-in-law. Very early one morning I was out in the kitchen spending time alone with the Lord, asking, "If I'm to speak, what am I to say?"

Suddenly my attention was caught by I Kings 20:28: "Thus saith the Lord, Because the Syrians have said, The Lord is God of the hills, but he is not God of the valleys, therefore will I deliver all this great multitude into thine hand and ye shall know that I am the Lord."

I was startled by the significance of what I read. The Syrians had gone down to defeat because they did not understand that God reigned in the valleys. Was not this the reason for the casualties in spiritual warfare—our failure to see God reigning in *all* circumstances, no matter how difficult?

There was a sense of spiritual adventure, as the Spirit of God illuminated that verse, revealing the spiritual principle involved. As of that moment, I knew two things: what I would be sharing Sunday morning, and that I was being given the key to truth which must later be shared in print. However, truth can be appropriated only when it is put to test and proven by experience. What I didn't know, was how soon the vernacular of the Spirit was to be translated into the valley experience.

The very next day I began hemorrhaging from my lungs more severely than I had in years. The coagulant the doctor gave me didn't seem to help much. Although I spent the week just resting, I was having bleeding spells around the clock. Nevertheless, I went ahead preparing for the Sunday service.

Yet I could not help but be aware of what I was up against. Since there was no pastor of the church at the time, the president of the board had called me. There could be no last-minute switch. I would be on the platform for an hour, speaking for at least half that time. After hemorrhaging, speaking for any protracted period is difficult, breathing an effort, my voice raspy.

As the weekend approached, I was no better. While nothing was said, I could sense in both our families the loving concern, the question unasked— What was I going to do?

All things considered, should I call and explain that illness would prevent my speaking? Somehow I just couldn't make that phone call.

On Sunday morning, I woke early with quite a bad spell of bleeding. But when my folks stopped by for us—the church being about a half-hour's drive to a nearby town—I was ready. Never did I feel I was making any climactic decision to "step out on faith." Nothing like that. The children of Israel moved when the cloud moved; and for me "the cloud" was moving.

At no time did I have the assurance all would be well. But neither was I afraid. As I sat looking out over the audience during the opening part of the service, there was that quiet confidence that since I had chosen to follow "the cloud," whatever happened now was God's responsibility.

We had discussed whether we should tell the one in charge about my physical problem before the service, in case I did have trouble. I had left that decision up to my husband. I never knew till later that he had decided that since we were trusting the Lord to see me through, we might just as well go all the way.

If I had needed proof that my decision was in accordance with God's will, I would have had it the moment I began to speak; my voice came forth clearly. Other than that, I was conscious of only one thing, the passion to communicate. I wanted so much for others to see the Lord reigning in their present circumstances, to realize that victory is contingent on recognizing His rule.

When I was little, Dad and I used to sing, "There's a church in the valley by the wildwood, the little brown church in the dale." When I thought about it later, I had to smile. Yes, this church was brown. But while it sat in the right angle of cement sidewalks, that Sunday, for me, in spiritual essence, it was deep "in the valley by the wildwood." For at the same time I was sharing what I'd discovered to be the way of victory in the valley experiences, I found I was on a reconnaissance mission to prove the territory could be taken.

Within an hour after we arrived home, I was bleeding again. But I had had no problem all the while we were at church, and I was very grateful.

What if I were to face the same situation again? I don't know. For I learned that even when identical situations recur, there is no established pattern, no answers by rote to the Spirit's direction. In every valley we need to know the King's directions for *that* crisis. Obedience will prove He is worthy of all our trust.

Knowing that the Lord reigns in the valleys is not just a matter of seeing that God says it, but encountering His doing over a lifetime. Knowing God, learning His ways, is something too big for any single experience—or multiplied experiences. The mountaintops are glorious, but by far the greater portion of our days are spent walking from "faith to faith" through the valleys.

Learning to know God is a way of life.

In spite of his staggering encounter with God on the road to Damascus, Paul had no "experience" fixation. He wasn't trapped in a spiritual treadmill, for he says, "Not as though I had already attained, either were already perfect; but I follow after . . ."[4]

So would I "follow after . . ."

What has ensued since I saw that God says that regardless of affliction or adversity, Jesus is Lord, has been both painful and exciting.

There have been "impossible" situations, heartache, tears. But as I have walked through these valleys, my confidence in the Lord has been established. Faith and trust have deepened their roots when lashed by the storm. And no matter how deep the hurt, there is the conscious joy of the indwelling Christ. Nowhere do I walk that I do not know the presence of the King.

Therefore I dare to pray, "No matter what valley experiences You have to lead me through, O God, teach me Your ways, establish me in righteousness, conquer me for Your Kingdom . . ."

And that is what He is doing, even in the poignant and challenging here-and-now.

"Blessed . . . is the man whom You discipline and instruct, O Lord, and teach out of Your law; That You may give him power to hold himself calm in the days of adversity." [1]

—*David*

2.

Lord of the Valleys

Bible verses are not isolated truths. Always they are a part of the whole revelation of the Eternal God—Father, Son, and Holy Spirit—through Scripture.

After the discovery of I Kings 20:28, I began to explore the setting in order to understand more clearly the implications of the Syrians' defeat in the valley. What were the parallels of practical application to our daily spiritual warfare? What were the facets that reflected light on the importance of accepting the Lordship of Jesus Christ in the valley experiences?

For 127,000 Syrians who fought under King Benhadad, it was the last mistake they would ever make, whittling God down to their finite understanding with their erroneous conjecture: "Their gods are gods of the hills; therefore they were stronger than we; but let us fight against them in the plain, and surely we shall be stronger than they." [2]

The Syrians did not deny the Being of God. That the Lord was God of the hills, they well understood; they were still licking the wounds of defeat. That this same God was also Lord of the valleys, they failed to recognize.

15

For a year they had chafed under the humility of being crushed by an army which they had embarrassingly outnumbered. Even so, they knew it was not the men of Israel who had caused their defeat; it had to be the God of Israel. Furthermore, every manifestation of His Being of which they knew, had taken place on a mountain. Consequently, a mental playback of all the events caused them to unanimously agree: they would fight Israel in the valley and they would win.

Their undoing was that they started with a half-truth, reasoning it through to what could only be an erroneous conclusion. At the same time they admitted the existence of God, they made Him less than God by denying His omnipresence; they did not see Him as being all places at all times. And so they went into battle, self-assured that this time they had everything going for them.

Sizing up the enemy dispelled the last doubt: "The children of Israel pitched before them like two little flocks of kids; but the Syrians filled the country." [3]

Yet both sides were about to learn experientially that neither the odds nor the field of combat mattered. According to His Word—regardless of anything—the battle was the Lord's.

And so it proved. That day saw 100,000 Syrian foot soldiers slain, and 27,000 more killed when God toppled a wall on those who fled. For the second time, the Syrians suffered a smashing defeat because they thought they could circumscribe the territory of God's dominion. To all who lived through the battle, He proved there are no boundaries; no man can set limits to the sphere where the One who is Lord of all realms rules.

But the truth is, we are just as guilty as the Syrians if we deny the omnipresence of God by failing to see Him reigning in all our circumstances. When the going really gets rough, how often do we groan, "Lord! You couldn't have anything to do with this!"

Until the Lordship of Jesus is more than theory, we will constantly be grappling with, and often be overwhelmed by, the distressing perplexities or fighting the adverse circumstances of life.

Before we can turn from our distress to God for deliverance, we must stop allocating His rule. Within, the battle will continue to rage as long as we attempt by our own strength to overcome our inadequacies, our bondages, our self-centeredness.

Only because they were rightly related to the Lord, did Israel come out on the winning side. Had they gone out to fight the Syrians simply as one army against another, the enemy would have mopped up the valley with them.

Even so, it is not enough to see God in control—we must be rightly related to the King.

When we are entrenched by the forces of the enemy—people who would cut us down, situations which would destroy us, or tragedy which would shake our faith—victory depends on who is our king. Is it Benhadad, who saw only the God of the hills? Or have we enlisted in the army of the King of kings, knowing that in whatever valley we find ourselves, the battle is His! And we are more than conquerors through Christ!

Who knew the God of the hills and the valleys like Elijah? He knew despondency, he knew despair, but he also knew his God. And his ultimate translation proves he didn't get mired down in the valleys.

It was Elijah who had the audacity to stipulate as God's judgment on the wicked rule of Ahab that there would not be the slightest trace of dew or rain in the land—according to His Word. And for thirty-six months no rain fell.

I recall how it is where I grew up on the western slopes of the "wet side" of the Cascades. Only a few weeks without rain brings the logging industry to an abrupt standstill. Just as soon as the humidity reaches a specified low, the area is declared a potential fire hazard. Men and trucks are immediately ordered out of the area; the woods and brush are tinder dry.

Imagine Samaria after three years without rain . . . the smell of dust . . . the parched dryness of the land . . . the people hungry and irritable, suffering all the miseries that carom around a land desolated by famine. And Ahab fuming with frustration that he could not lay hands on Elijah; he saw nothing but the prophet as the source of the nation's distress. The nation's sin, he didn't even consider.

At long last, face to face with Elijah, he exploded.

"Art thou he that troubleth Israel?"

Elijah quickly set the record straight: "Not me, Ahab. You're the guilty one, you and your rotten household. Don't blame me for God's judgment when you've turned your back on His laws to go chasing after the gods of Baal. Go gather your prophets and all the people and meet me at Mount Carmel."

Elijah had no long sermon. It wasn't needed, for the eternal question he posed demands an immediate decision: "How long halt ye between two opinions? if the Lord be God, follow him: but if Baal, then follow him."

Nothing but silence from the grandstand; they thought to play it safe, like many today who think they can be noncommittal to this question.

Not so, the prophet. Declaring himself to be the only remaining prophet of the Lord, he challenged, "Let two bullocks be slain, wood lain, but no fire kindled by man . . . then call on the name of the Lord: and the God that answereth by fire, let him be God."

Four hundred and fifty, in desperate frenzy, slashed themselves, had hysterics, tried everything the flesh could conjure. While their frantic religious activity raised clouds of dust, their gods remained aloof, unmoved by the commotion. And all throughout the day, this miserable, evil bunch of men, soaked with sweat, dirty, bloody, and panic-stricken, were relentlessly subjected to Elijah's mockery.

In contrast was Elijah's calm as he took command. Sullenly, the crowd shifted over to assist as he directed. Elijah's every act was deliberate; the setting of the stones to repair the altar . . . the digging of the trench around it . . . the placing of the wood . . . the preparation of the bullock . . . and so there would never be a question left in anyone's mind, the soaking of the sacrifice with twelve barrels of water. When the trench was full to the brim, the well-sodden sacrifice was ready.

Elijah's confidence was twofold: his relationship to the Lord, and that he had done none of this on his own initiative. Raising his eyes, he reminded the Lord, "I am thy servant, and I have done all these things at thy word." This was the basis for his faith to pray, "Hear me, O Lord, hear me, that this people may know that thou art the Lord God."

The Scripture bears record: "Then the fire of the Lord fell!" Bullock, wood, even the stones of the altar, were consumed, the trenches left dry!

And suddenly the people became very spiritual.

Let people behold the supernatural and they'll be quick to clamor, "The Lord, He is God!" even as this vacillating lot. But never make the mistake of assuming that vocal acclamation alone is faith.

Listening to their belated testimony, Elijah remonstrated: "Not enough! Baptism by water and baptism by fire aren't all there is to affirming His Lordship. The false prophets must be slain." [4]

When God deals with His people, His mode may vary, but it will always be according to certain basic principles. God deals in totalities. He accepts nothing less than total commitment, total allegiance. Elijah gave them to know that whatever evil had turned them away from God must be totally destroyed.

Of Jesus, John says, "For this purpose the Son of God was manifested, that he might destroy the works of the devil." [5] It is still His purpose. He will not manifest Himself as Lord until all the "false prophets" have been dealt with. Jesus desires to search out every sin, every ungodly thing to which we would cling, that He might deal it a deathblow.

Have you ever considered why the false prophets were destroyed, and yet others, just as guilty of worshiping Baal, were spared? The prophets who were slain were a symbol: they claimed supernatural power while acting in the flesh. Their fate is surely a warning to those who would dare to do likewise.

Elijah saw that all the false prophets were put to death. But still the people were without water, and Elijah accepted the responsibility to do something about it.

Faith, stimulated by obedience, "heard" the sound of abundance of rain, even before he began his climb back up the mountain. Nonetheless, he assumed a position of humility on his face before the Lord, to pray—seven times—until a cloud the size of a man's hand was reported rising out of the sea. That was enough for Elijah; he knew it was time to take cover—and fast!

The sky blackened, the wind roared, faith ripped open the heavens, pulled the stoppers from the clouds, and the parched earth was drenched again.[6]

Two miracles wrought on Mount Carmel by God through His servant: on the mountaintop Elijah ministered to God; on the mountaintop he set the stage for the Lord to demonstrate His power. Faith, obedience, and prayer were the backdrops.

But what follows? Who would have expected to find Elijah so soon in the valley, in the wilderness under a juniper tree?

When 450 were missing from the queen's table that night, the queen was furious. The prophet who dared to mock 450 madmen, who condemned King Ahab to his face, when threatened by Jezebel turned heel to escape to the valley. And what a wilderness he found himself in!

A day's journey beyond where he had left his servant, alone and exhausted, he reached the limit of his strength. That was precisely where God wanted him!

With terrible anguish, he was overcome by the inane course of his action. In his remorse, Elijah made a discovery: within himself were exactly the same human weaknesses which God loathed in his fathers; he was no better than they. Shaken to the core by this bit of self-discovery, he pleaded with God to let him die.

I used to wonder how it was that I could know God manifest in the miraculous, the soaring of my faith to such extreme heights, the surety that nothing could keep me from believing God for anything—and then, come the very next test, I would panic and react quite like Elijah. All I lacked was the juniper tree.

Then I made a discovery. The psalmist says that God "remembers . . . we are dust." [7] God also wants us to remember, never to forget. He will send circumstance after circumstance to show us what we really are, and therefore where our dependency must always be centered.

God ignored Elijah's wail, his moaning to die. He wasn't in the least shaken by Elijah's reaction to self-discovery. His prophet had faithfully ministered to Him on the mountaintop. Now He purposely pressed Elijah into the valley where, stripped and desolate, he had no recourse but to receive from the Lord.

It is God's way to thus expose our weaknesses, and then to begin to minister to us at the level of our immediate need.

So it was God gave Elijah sleep. Then after he had rested awhile, an angel touched him, talked to him, supplied bread and water.

Have you ever felt the pure touch of love: an arm about your shoulder, a handclasp—or heard the voice of God's love through the lips of a saint when you were in the valley of utter despair? Or have you known God's provision for physical needs ministered through the human hands of one of His servants, often one from whom you least expected help? I have. And always, I knew it was God reminding me that I was never beyond the reach of His love.

God's complete provision was so beyond the ordinary in that wilderness valley that Elijah "went in the strength of that meat forty days and forty nights unto Horeb the mount of God." [8]

More than once I've been told I've been living on "borrowed time." My answer: "Who isn't?" Every breath we take is from God, and we are always only one breath away from eternity—the last one. We are all living on borrowed time. But never forget—God has the last word!

Elijah still hadn't learned this. Running from those who sought to slay him, he crawled back into a cave to hide, rather than asking, "What next Lord? And where to?" He should have been more frightened of moving outside the center of God's will than of a knife at his throat.

Is this the "mighty prophet of the Lord" furtively encamped in a cave? Terrified for his life? Mistakenly thinking he alone has not bowed to Baal?

But the Lord understood; He knew precisely Elijah's problem—Elijah just didn't understand what had been happening to him down in the valleys. And so God commanded him to go out and stand on the mount of the Lord. He had something to teach him.

With a mighty wind God rent the mountain, rattled the rocks as marbles in a small boy's hand, and emblazoned the reeling spectacle with fingers of fire. Elijah's knuckles were colorless as he clutched his mantle. Then he heard what was scarcely more than a whisper. It was God . . .

Elijah, you saw the power of God when fire consumed the sacrifice, also in the wind and the rain when the famine was broken. Now you have discovered I am not in the wind, the fire, nor the earthquake—but in the still small voice. Elijah, Elijah, you haven't learned to communicate with Me in the absence of the dramatic yet! Whoever would serve Me, must learn this lesson. And the classroom is the wilderness valley.

It is the same today. Some have sought after and majored on the dramatic until their spiritual hearing has become desensitized to the still small voice of a holy God who whispers His most precious truths to those who in quietness listen and are able to hear in spite of the din.

Still Elijah was reluctant to leave the safety of the cave. Trying to protect his own life when God ordered him back down to the wilderness to fulfill his duties as a prophet, he forfeited the assurance of God's protection.

God had more to say: "Elijah, you aren't the only one! There are seven thousand faithful besides you." [9]

Have you seen them, or have you been guilty yourself, a Christian scrunched down moodily under his own private juniper tree, or withdrawn into a cave of self-righteousness, so taken up with your "sole spirituality" you don't know about the other seven thousand either, refusing even to acknowledge them if they feed in the pasture on the other side of the fence some man has erected?

Many have had genuine dealings with God on the mountaintop, but they're still trying to live on past experience. They've never let God work out those things in their lives which He can accomplish only in the valley experiences. They just don't understand about the valleys.

Elijah had found it exciting on the mountaintop, but mighty distressing when in the valley he began to discover himself as God knew him. The farther he went into the wilderness valley, however, the greater was his revelation of God—not in the supernatural miraculous power as when consuming fire struck the sacrifice, but in that inner communion that centers in the character of God.

Under the juniper, exhausted and without food and water, Elijah knew God's full provision; in the cave, scared for his life, he learned that God has the last word; in the gale, with the earth shaking beneath his feet, he heard the hush of God's voice. And cringing in self-righteousness, self-pity, and fear, he is made to know that God is not without a remnant in the land. God is still God, and there is no place where He is not God—the all-powerful, all-knowing, ever-present Eternal God.

Until we come to grips with the legitimate claim Jesus Christ has to be Lord of our life, we'll continue to chafe at life's distresses without ever coming to know God's ways.

Jesus will never step into a situation uninvited, but to those who seek to know Him, He has promised to reveal Himself.

Jesus said it was revelation which caused Peter to recognize Him as "the Christ, the Son of the living God." [10] But it was Peter's verbal confession that indeed Jesus was the Anointed One come to rule which began to release the operation of the Spirit to make these words life to him.

We see the same principle in operation at creation. First, a vision. Then, the spoken Word. And immediately, that which God declared was!

Ours must be the same confession, both with the mouth and in the spirit. But before it becomes our own, revelation must always be translated into a working principle in our lives.

Peter's message on the day of Pentecost was born of God. Furthermore, in the power of the Holy Spirit, he could say with all honesty, "Hearken to my words," [11] for Truth had become his through the reality of experience.

Declaring, "Whosoever shall call on the name of the Lord shall be saved," [12] he remembered how it was: the black waters of Galilee swirling up around him; his garments clinging to his body; the fear which gripped his being—it was a long way to shore; echoing in his memory, his own frantic cry, "Lord, save me!" [13] Again he feels the pressure of the Master's hand lifting him, grasping his hand as they walked together now, back across the water to the boat where the others waited . . . and watched.

Only the familiarity of that Voice had given Peter the courage to climb out of the boat. Though it had been a frightening experience, he would always be glad he hadn't waited behind with the others.

And because it happened to him, he could make the spiritual application, words put to test in the darkness of the night which ring with reality. For Peter knew that no matter how far a man had sunk in sin, Jesus would never ignore that cry . . . "Lord, save me!"

It had taken a lot of blundering on Peter's part before the Lordship of Jesus Christ became not only the confession of his lips, but the motivating force of his life. He knew the valleys dark and deep . . . but in them, he came to know his Lord.

To know Jesus as Lord is to know the presence, the power, and the provision of the King in every circumstance, in our present need.

When Jesus spoke of the Abundant Life,[14] He was not looking into the eternities. He was not talking about a quality of life, futuristic or passive. For the Abundant Life in Christ doesn't begin on the other side of physical death. It is the here-and-now of the Gospel, the coming in of the King of Glory through the Calvary-rent veil into the holy of holies of the human heart—to reign.

But we will never know this dimension of life until we tear down the "no trespassing" signs in those areas where we've never before allowed the Lord to enter. Every gate must be unlatched from the inside and thrown wide open, the Lord of Glory given complete access to saturate the human spirit with the Holy Spirit of God. When God indwells His temple, He will transform a life of passive existence or frustrated activity into victorious participation.

Jesus confronted the disciples with the immediacy of faith. "Do you *now* believe?" [15] "*Now* is My Kingdom!" [16] "The hour . . . *now* is, when the dead shall hear the voice of the Son of God: and they that hear shall live." [17] Whenever God speaks to a receptive heart, life flows.

Heaven? Of course! That follows. But the moment we enthrone Jesus Christ as Lord, God becomes our Dwelling Place. In perfect safety, our feet upon a sure path, we can walk *today* with Jesus, and keep walking right out into the eternities.

Jude so beautifully blends the present and the future aspect of the Kingdom in His invocation: "And *now*—all glory to him who alone is God, who saves us through Jesus Christ our Lord; yes, splendor and majesty, all power and authority are his from the beginning; his they are and his they evermore shall be. And he is able to keep you from slipping and falling away, and to bring you, sinless and perfect, into his glorious presence with mighty shouts of everlasting joy." [18]

For every Christian, Jesus bears just one receipt. It is those marks of the Cross—whether He redeemed us from a mansion or the gutter, the cost was exactly the same—His outpoured life. Those marks are also His claim to rule those He has redeemed. Therefore we are cheating Him unless we are willing to relinquish the right to rule our own life.

I've had to face it; whenever I give place to self-pity, resentment, pride, fear, or merely a negative attitude, I'm denying the Lordship of Jesus.

Yielding to His authority, though, I've discovered, doesn't restrict the spirit. On the contrary, with every new area of life brought under His rule, there is a tremendous release from the littleness of self-rule into the unfathomable sovereign-rule of God. He takes over when we stop struggling to cling to our own way, to self-defense, self-righteousness, self-rights, self-rule, or to perpetuate self in any way.

The Lord doesn't just issue commands and then stand back while we flounder around trying to carry them out in our own strength. He is a dynamo of power manifest through the Holy Spirit.

However, Jesus never said it would be easy. He guarantees a Cross to carry; He promises there will be persecution, misunderstanding, loneliness, no rights to anything of our own.

Still it is in the deepest valleys I've come to expect the greatest manifestation of the glory of His presence, His power, and His provision.

Even as the Syrians found there was no limit to the area where God rules, I've come to discover in the valley experiences that we can't build a frame around the Lordship of Jesus Christ! Before the glue is dry, the Lord will reveal new areas of our life to which He has claim. But as we surrender them to Him, choosing by attitude and action to affirm our faith in the absolute authority of Christ standing over every situation, we find the horizons in God are limitless. In the high places or the low, we can know the infinite dimension of abundant living. And it matters not what is going on around us.

Psalm 40

"Why do you say, O Jacob, and speak, O Israel, 'My way is hid from the Lord, and my right is disregarded by my God'? Have you not known? Have you not heard? . . . I, the Lord your God, hold your right hand. . . . I will open rivers on the bare heights, and fountains in the midst of the valleys. . . ." [1]

—Isaiah

3.

Why the Valleys?

Have you been taught that you must never ask "Why?" of the Lord? No matter what happens, you mustn't question God's purpose?

I'd so often heard the axiom, "Faith does not question 'Why?'" that for years I missed much of what God endeavored to teach me through the difficult experiences of life. I actually thought it was a sin to seek to know why He had taken me down into this or that valley. It being gross unbelief, it wasn't for me to understand.

Of course, God in His mercy and love still re-directed my thinking and wrought changes in my course of action. But certainly never to the full extent He could have, had I believed He intended for me to know why He allowed certain things to happen.

How can God accomplish the ultimate in discipline, chastening, or in teaching me His ways, if He leaves me in the dark as to what He is seeking to do? I would say now that it is nothing less than irrational *not* to ask, "Lord, what are You saying to me in this situation which You've allowed?"

True, questioning can denote lack of faith or trust, but be assured, when it does, it's the motive that is wrong, not the asking.

Two obvious motives may prompt our asking. Both are easily observed in children when they have been asked or forbidden to do a certain thing. There may be that contemptuous retort: "Why should I?" That's the spirit of rebellion. But if I ask my son to go to the store for me, I expect a "Why?" That's the spirit of cooperation. If he is to accomplish my purpose in sending him, he must know what I want.

Even so, if we are to cooperate intelligently and by choice with His will and His workings, we need to know at least something of what God wants.

Sometimes He may not tell us everything we'd like to know at once. But if we keep our hearts open—faith accepting what we do not understand as His working—He will communicate what He is trying to work in us through the circumstances of the moment. And life's conflicts become spiritual adventures once God begins to clue us in to the what and why of the valleys.

Above all, we will begin to fulfill the passion of God's heart as we come to know Him. For the valleys, first of all, are that we might discover God.

Jesus Christ is the ever-existing verification of God's desire to reveal Himself. Although God's desire to communicate Himself to His creation is built into the very structure of the universe, substantiated by Scripture, and evidenced in all of nature, it is expressly revealed in the Son, God accommodating Himself to the Person of Jesus, not only to redeem us, but that we might relate to God as a Person. The very purpose in the Holy Spirit taking the things of Jesus and making them ours,[2] is that there will be reciprocal communion with the Father.

God is so determined to communicate, if nothing else avails, He will take desperate measures, even to permitting the dark and battering storms which leave us breathless and shaken. After we've flailed around in the blackness, exhausted from trying to get our bearings, we'll stop our sputtering and listen. If we know from whence cometh our help,[3] all our senses strain to hear His voice. As He begins to speak, if we listen with an ear to obeying, we'll find light dispelling the darkness.

To "pray without ceasing," [4] is to know constant communication, something more than a running commentary of "bless mes" and "gimmes," liberally sprinkled with "Praise the Lords." And not religious exercises either.

If we are to know what God is seeking to do in the valley experiences, the door of communication must swing both ways. It's imperative to learn to know the voice of the One who is Lord of our lives!

What does it take?

There must be a predisposed determination to obedience preceding any revelation of God. Needed also, is a quiet spirit and God-consciousness.

We won't learn to discern the voice of God by getting our friends to storm heaven in our behalf. Nor by our own frantic emergency requisitions.

Not that we don't need the prayers of others. But not so that God will give *us* an answer, except perhaps for confirmation, rather that *we* will open up to God that we might hear what He is saying. While we may receive much from God because of others' prayers, we will never learn to know God's voice until we seek Him for ourselves.

In the valley, too broken to do anything but drop at His feet and cry, "Lord!" we won't be distracted when He speaks.

Jesus often interspersed His teaching with, "He that hath ears to hear, let him hear." [5] We "hear" when there is that completeness of surrender and unqualified commitment to obedience which allows His Spirit so to permeate our whole being that His voice becomes an inner conscious and poignant awareness of His will.

Communication with God is really getting through, the interrelating of my spirit with the Holy Spirit, until there is a harmony of my spirit with the Spirit of God that diffuses throughout my whole being.

Once we come to a personal discovery of God, the valleys will begin to disclose how totally dependent we are upon the Shepherd. Thus they serve also to teach us dependence upon God.

Mountaintop experiences tend to make us react as if we had all the answers, just like Peter did when he started telling the Lord what they should do: "Let's get with it, Lord! Let's build three tabernacles on the spot!" Had this impetuous fisherman thought it through, I doubt that he'd have considered being involved in the building of one tabernacle, let alone three. But then perhaps he'd figured Jesus would agree it was a great idea, and the tabernacles would appear as miraculously as the prophets did.

So it is, far too often, when we are on the mountaintop, we are so sure we know exactly what service God would appreciate, specifically what needs doing, how many committees we need—or we may even strive for a new "record of faith" in our one-man sloop, just to show the world. We want it known what we have experienced, what we have seen, what we know about God.

But boxed in the valley, our independence is swallowed up in the lengthening shadows. We are not so smugly sure of ourselves when we can't see even a small patch of clear sky to get our bearings. But we're much more ready to accept the fact that we need the Shepherd's leading, that we need to hear His voice.

The emphasis in the valley is not on what we have witnessed, but realizing our total dependence upon Jesus—breath by breath. Not what has been, but what is.

For years I sought an experience which would make me a jet-propelled Christian; if the Lord would but set the auto-pilot, I would continuously soar to spiritual heights above the clouds.

Soar I did. But I found spiritual altitude never becomes fixed. After a good many crash landings, I came to realize it was a very stupid pilot indeed who tried to fly continuously without refilling his fuel supply or having his plane serviced. Stupid and bound to perish.

No spiritual experience ever makes the valleys unnecessary, for in them, we are forced to draw daily on the resources of God.

I used to say, "Whenever we reach the limit of our resources, the Lord stands close by to supply our every need." Now I'm learning that total dependency means that I start out with His supply, not holding anything apart as mine.

Having begun our discovery of God and beginning to learn dependence upon Him, we find the discipline and dealings of God are also received in the valley experiences.

In certain adjustments and lessons we have to learn, God in His wisdom does not accomplish everything in one cataclysmic experience, nor in two or three, for many reasons.

Make no mistake, though the process leading up to our new life in Christ may be drawn out, we are born into the family of God in a crisis which takes place in a moment. Jesus said, "You cannot serve two masters." [6] There's a dividing line between the two; the crisis comes when we step over that line to begin to serve God. In an instant of time, God does the miraculous in transforming a life, breaking bondages, healing bodies.

But the Christian life is more than a succession of crisis experiences. Once we have become sons of God, there is the growing up into maturity—and not without some spiritual growing pains.

Know that the dealings of God are a day-by-day discipline; it is life. Experiences are important. Being born of the Spirit is imperative. But Christianity is a life to be lived in Christ daily! And by far the greatest expanse of living lies between the mountaintops; the disciplining experiences transpire in the valley.

Jesus did not transform the men who were to become the spiritual fathers of the New Testament church in one single dramatic episode. He taught them discipline. For three-and-a-half years He trudged the dusty roads, over mountains, through valleys, in storm, in want; in every conceivable circumstance. They saw him minister to all men—the lepers, the demon-possessed, the harlots, the ecclesiastical dignitaries. They noted He separated Himself from no one—the rich, the poor, the respected, the scorned—whatever their need. By His touch and His teaching, He showed Himself to be the Answer.

In all He did, He was putting the chosen twelve through a conditioning process. They were not just hobnobbing with nice people, the elite, but right out in the hard realistic ruggedness of life being lived daily with Him, they were rubbing shoulders with all of humanity's woes.

No five-minute overhaul job would have prepared them for what lay ahead. Nor would the lessons be over when He left them to return to His Father.

So deeply ingrained in Jewish hearts was the necessity to have the kingdom of Israel restored that even the disciples were still clinging to the hope that this would culminate Christ's ministry after the resurrection. But it was not to be. Their hope was shattered, their dreams blasted; the Messiah was not to become King of an earthly kingdom.

They had known dark valleys—the darkest of all the day the One in whom they had placed all their hopes hung on the Cross, His form lifeless, distorted, horrible to look upon. The days which followed were desolate, their dreams now displaced with doubt and despair.

God's time clock had been set for the outpouring of the Holy Spirit. They had not been told when. They had only been told where. And that they must wait.

Waiting is never easy. But to feel the call of God upon the heart and then to hear God say, "Wait!" can be terribly frustrating. People say, "I thought you were going to Bible school, to seminary, to the mission field, to enter a new field of labor. What are you still doing here? When are you going? What is the matter?" And all one can say is, "The Lord says, 'Wait.' "

Once when we were under the discipline of such an experience, God spoke to me so clearly through Eccles. 3:14, 17, that I not only saw God's time clock, but "waiting" as it related to perfection and permanence in all God does.

It should not be hard to understand why we need the valleys of discipline when we read that Jesus Himself learned obedience to the Father by the things which He suffered. What He imparts to us, He has known experientially. Consequently, we have the assurance that we can't go any place He hasn't been before. No matter what, He knows. And more than that, He's the Source of whatever we need in our time of trouble—even the Spirit of obedience that we may do the Father's will.

Because Jesus yielded Himself to death, it had no control over Him. Through the act of submission, He retained the power of life. Submission becomes our means of appropriating the very source of power which brought Jesus forth from the tomb . . . even for the quickening of the mortal body.

Since I have come to understand more fully the reasons for the valley experiences, over and over I have been utterly broken as I remember how violently I have struggled against some of the most glorious things God was trying to do. It took me so long to apprehend what the valleys were all about, and to realize that in struggling against God's discipline and dealings in them I was struggling against the greatest love I have ever known. Selfish and self-willed, I regarded submission as a sign of weakness; I was still determined to retain some control over my own life; I was willing to do anything but submit.

Often when I thought that at last I was learning to accept the circumstances, there would begin the bitterest struggle of all. I had yet to concede that submission is power.

Even when there is that inward confession, I have found myself acting independently. But God continues to work until that confession does control our actions.

In the Book of Job, Elihu gives us beautiful and graphic descriptions of the natural forces exerted in the universe. Not only does he declare God's exclusive control, but he outlines how they effect

His purposes. Of the storms, he says, "He causeth it to come whether for correction, or for His land, or for mercy." [7]

There are parallels for the storms which lash the spirit. In the valleys of discipline, for correction: to right wrong actions and attitudes. Even as physical storms are for the land—rain, snow, and freezing replenish the soil, making it fertile and restoring the land to fruitfulness—so through the dealings of God comes the renewing of our spirit that we may bring to fruition His purposes. And even as the physical storms which cause destruction are not without mercy, in that thus nature is kept in balance, even so is His mercy extended to us in the dealings of God. In love and mercy, through the breaking experiences, God seeks to destroy those things within which would otherwise destroy us.

Being conformed to the image of God's Son demands identification. And identification with Jesus can mean nothing less than being motivated by the same principles which motivated Him. He offered Himself to the Father to be made Broken Bread. And if we are to be used to feed the multitude, we likewise need to offer ourselves for the breaking experiences.

When David prayed, "Create in me a clean heart, O God: and renew a right spirit within me," [8] he knew it would be accomplished only through brokenness. For his prayer continues, "The sacrifices of God are a broken spirit: a broken and a contrite heart, O God, thou wilt not despise." [9]

The word "contrite" here has the connotation of being literally crushed to powder.

We can't do it alone. Neither can God. We are told to take up our Cross. But never is it inferred that we should wield the hammer which sinks the nails through hands and feet; the driving of the last nail would be impossible. While we must embrace the principle of brokenness, there must also be the divine operation of God if the attitude of brokenness produces actions and attitudes pleasing to Him.

When Jesus wanted to feed the five thousand, the bread was first broken in His hands. Even so, know that we are in His hands in the breaking process.

Jesus said to Pilate, "Thou couldst have no power at all against me, except it were given thee from above." [10] When Christ indwells our being, neither can anything break us except as God allows. But being indwelt by Him, we must arrive at the experiences of brokenness because of our identity with Him.

If you've met some issue head-on and come out of the collision broken, but more than conqueror through Christ, then when you minister, it will truly be as broken bread. If someone else is having a struggle with the same issue or one with a similar principle involved, because you have been obedient and ready to die to your "rights," as you minister, the supernatural happens. The truth you speak becomes vitally alive. In reality, by the Spirit of God, it does become a Living Word, because you are ministering broken bread and poured-out wine.

Always one should be careful not to minister just the experience, for there is the danger of self being inflated. But if we minister because we've had an experience, God will use our death through that experience, to bring His life to another, and Jesus, not self, will be glorified.

There must come the breaking of the vessel of our humanity before light can break forth to reveal the treasure within—the Abiding Christ within the human spirit and personality. If this is what we really want, God will adjust His tactics, whatever it takes, to accomplish the breaking. His means are varied.

He often breaks us parents through our children. Someone has said, "If you want to find out whether or not you are sanctified, just let someone touch your children." I say, "If you want to know whether your commitment to His Lordship is for real, just let *God* start touching your children."

However, it is possible to go through the breaking process and still give forth no light. If we retain those things pertaining to darkness—slip easily into little dishonesties, slander, gossip, impurity—

we'll have nothing but dark shadows to emit when there is any breaking. And the world isn't looking for shadows; it seeks light. When my world comes crashing down around me, when Jesus is bringing me low, when I am being trampled inside, I can know this is the Lord allowing all that would cloud the reflection of the beauty of Jesus in my life to be destroyed.

Through the dealings of God in the valleys, there is the further working out of our identity with Christ. It is so important as we touch other's lives. Paul assures us that as we are comforted by God in all our tribulations, so we are able to comfort others in their times of trouble.

The cry of God's heart through Isaiah was, "Comfort ye, comfort ye my people . . ." [11] But unless we have walked the same road before, our words of intended comfort can be so empty they hurt more than they help. However, if we have known God's comfort in our hour of need, we have something real to give because it is a part of us.

Have you prayed that your life would bless others? Then you have asked to be enrolled in God's school where the lessons are very practical, for to receive everything in a package-deal would never equip us to minister to others who are going through deep trials.

It is not enough to know identification with Christ. We must be able to identify with human need.

Once as I prayed, "That I may know him, and the power of his resurrection, and the fellowship of his sufferings, being made conformable unto his death," [12] the Lord let me know that the experiences I had been going through were my dues and identification card into that fellowship—the reality of total identity with my Lord!

Recently, when I couldn't seem to get above the pressure of a certain situation, I spent an unplanned half-hour with the mother of a retarded child. This woman had known a great deal of heartache, but her quiet devotion to Jesus shone through all she said that afternoon. I came away feeling lifted by that brief time with her.

So it is, in the darkness of the valley, let one who has crowned Jesus Lord of his life at the time his heart was breaking, speak, and I'll be quick to listen. But the voice of one who has only theory without experience to offer often leaves me cold.

Another reason I have found for the valley experiences is that God wants to expand our faith. He does so by putting us into those "impossible" situations which would drive us to despair—except that our faith is exercised to see the Lord work to change the impossible or to change us.

The experience of Peter, James, and John on the Mount of Transfiguration was astounding. Not only did Moses and Elijah appear, but though they had been dead for generations, it seems no introductions were necessary. Apparently the disciples knew them instantly!

But no one can remain on the mountaintop forever. Inevitably those transcendent moments passed, and it was time for them to go back down to the valley.

On the mountain peak they had witnessed the Son of God revealed in His glory. But at the foot of the mountain was revealed to them the reason for man's inability to meet human need.

It was a painfully realistic problem—an anguished father with his demon-possessed son. Both had suffered years of torment by the evil spirit which racked the boy's body, at times throwing him into the fire. Except for what little he could do to protect the boy from injury, the father was helpless.

When the man began telling Jesus that the disciples had been unable to cast out the demon, no doubt humiliated and ashamed, they tried to press back into the crowd. But they had truly wanted to help. Why had they failed?

"This kind goeth not out but by prayer and fasting," [13] Jesus told them. In the valley, they were challenged to a release of faith effected only through self-discipline and self-denial.

When I read, "For so is the will of God, that with well doing ye may put to silence the ignorance of foolish men," [14] I began to understand another purpose for the valley experiences. If we allow the Lord to rule in them, there is created faith to demonstrate and declare His Lordship to the world.

I know that whatever the situation, God wants my "well doing" —my actions and reactions—to be a testimony to the world, for it is our testimony to His Lordship in the valleys that counts for real with both God and man. I don't know how it will be with you; I only know how it has been with me.

I helped care for the dearest friend I ever had, during the eight weeks she suffered the agony of death by toxemia, until at the last, when she was totally blind and semiconscious, her screams could be heard from the hospital parking lot. She was one whose whole life had been completely committed to her Lord. I held her baby in my arms and wept as I thought how she had asked me to pray with her that this child might be conceived, the child whose birth had taken her life and left a heartbroken husband and three little motherless boys.

Two days before she left us, I woke early in the morning, picked up my New Testament close by and read, "I go to my Father. . . . If ye loved me, ye would rejoice!" [15] It was as if she had spoken. And it was then I knew . . . Though I could not stop the tears, I could say, "Yes, Lord . . . and I do rejoice."

Her oldest son went through his own lonely Gethsemane at the time. And later he struggled to accept the One who holds the keys of life and death. Why did God take his mother if He is love? A few years later, fifteen years old now, he stood beside his mother's grave at Easter and prayed, "Because of the message we heard this morning, Lord, we thank You that there is nothing here." Could a theologian have put it so well?

Four months before our little girl was born, my husband was critically injured in an explosion. During the difficult days that followed, I received a letter from a dear friend. I had met May and Neal Johnson shortly after their only son, Joe, was killed in Germany during World War II. They had been "Mama and Papa J" to our youth group. Even though their hearts must often have been breaking, they lavished their love on us and were concerned about and interested in everything we did.

The day after my husband was hurt, I received word that Neal had died of a heart attack. Hearing about Al's accident, May wrote me at once, encouraging me to be brave and "a real witness to others that you have a Lord who supplies all your needs."

She continued, "Somehow, dating back to our Joe's going, I have felt that at no other time could we be a better witness before others, and so I was able to 'smile back at God' when He called my dear Neal home. He and I had such a perfectly wonderful understanding about God's calling us home; we knew it was far better. Of course I am lonely—oh, so lonely—but I can count my blessings." [16]

I counted mine too, and one was knowing May. She not only believed Jesus was Lord, but by her "well-doing"—her actions and reactions—she bore witness that He reigned as King in the valley of her sorrow. And in what I was going through, she encouraged me to do likewise.

Having no reason to suspect it held gasoline, my husband had been opening a supposedly empty steel drum with a welding torch. I was shielded from what happened till Al was on his way to the hospital. After I had been told and was waiting to go to the hospital myself, there was that inner knowing that his condition was critical. Yet there was no panic. I knew only the wonder of being wrapped in God's love, while over and over the words repeated themselves: "God is love! God is good! God can be trusted!" These were absolutes and my strength and comfort in that hour, although I had no assurance that Al would live.

A phone call in the night; a near-fatal auto accident; two boys whose lives were spared only by the mercy of the Lord. One was our son. Cut keenly into my memory is that long tortuous ride to the hospital in the early morning hours, the uncertainty of life or death, suffering with them in their pain and remorse. Yet through those desperate hours there was that assurance which kept me calm and at peace within, knowing *all* things were in His hands. That incomprehensible peace which even then caused me to lift my heart godward, to say with confidence, "Yes, Lord—to all You have allowed. I know You are in full control."

Surely one of the Lord's greatest desires is that we may know and share with others that no matter how dark the valley, "in the night, His song will be with me." [17] Even when our sobbing muffles the song, the song is there—if He is Lord.

The conflicts of life, the bitter thrusts, the deep hurts, misunderstanding—other experiences much too personal to share, but all valley experiences where we meet the claims of His Lordship— these bring the test of our faith, not the test of our experience. And faith praises, no matter what.

No doubt anyone could have been stirred to praise seeing Jesus and the prophets talking together, transfigured in translucent light, just as we may be quick to exalt God when we have been blessed with some miraculous manifestation, provision, or God's gift of salvation. But what about those times when He in love and wisdom withholds His ready supply to our earnest supplication? Do we moan and groan and carry on as though we've been forgotten and forsaken by the Lord? Do we blame the church or ourselves for lack of faith, or even begin to doubt His care?

If so, our reactions prove that we need the valleys; we need to pray, "Teach me Your ways!"

What is our response when we have to work from an empty cupboard? When the payments on the mortgage are past due, the bills piling up, the paycheck has stopped, and there is no job to be had? How is it when there's an emptiness of heart and an empty place at the table? When we've been deeply hurt by the one we love most? When those from whom we seek comfort have nothing but criticism to give?

The testimony which carries an impact is the voice of praise and thanksgiving which rises above the storm.

No, it doesn't always come spontaneously. That's why we are told to offer the sacrifice of praise—a sacrifice costs us something. And sometimes praise is harder to part with than our last nickel!

Why the valleys?

". . . it is God which worketh in you both to will and to do of his good pleasure." [18]

Everything God does, everything He allows, every valley He drops us into, has divine purpose. As a dear elderly pioneer-missionary friend used to say, "God doesn't experiment with any of His children." What He does, He does with calculated reason.

If you ask the Lord to do a specific work in your life, be prepared; He'll arrange the circumstances which alone will accomplish the necessary changes.

One thing, though, we must understand. It isn't the valley experience in itself that renews a right spirit within us, that conforms us to the image of His Son, that glorifies Jesus. People go through terrible ordeals and gain nothing of spiritual value. The change God is able to work in us in the valleys is contingent upon our acceptance, our surrender, our total cooperation with the Spirit of God, our confidence that He always goes before, and what we commit, He keeps.

Nowhere does God promise protection for what is not committed to Him, for that which we clasp in *our* hand. But He takes full responsibility for that which we place in *His* hand.

Why the valleys?

They are inevitable if we choose to walk with God. We can't stand on the mountaintop and walk very far without going down to the valley—unless we walk in circles.

Some people talk about taking a step of faith. But faith is not a step, it is a walk. Faith will take you into the valleys—for faith walks with God.

A credit manager of many years observed, "You can never tell what a man will do till the pressure is applied."

We will have to take the blessings of the mountaintop into the valley of human experience. This is the proving ground for our allegiance to the King of kings.

Repeating the pledge of allegiance to the flag is one thing; fighting on the battlefield for the country which that flag represents—and dying there—is something else. The ping of the enemy's bullets—as he attacks with doubt, discouragement, distress, and despair—don't let us forget: we are in a spiritual battle that is for real. Our verbal commitment to Jesus as Lord must be sealed by the laying down of our life—the sum total of all our relationships and rights—in the midst of the conflict. Only then will we know the power of His resurrected life—the abundant life that is ours in Christ.

Whatever you are going through, know that the most formidable valleys will become spiritually productive as in them you discover God, learn dependence upon Him, know His discipline and dealings, that you might demonstrate and declare His Lordship.

In the darkest night, there will be the expanding of vision, the illumination of understanding, and the glory of His presence, as God begins to unfold His eternal purposes. He will begin to give you some answers, even as it is written, "Surely the Lord God does nothing, without revealing His secret to His servants." [19]

So I have found it. And it has been in the conflict of living that I have come to know each moment is guided and guarded by the Lord. Not with any sense of "having arrived," but out of the wonder of His love, I want to go on to share with you how God brought meaning into some desperately difficult valley experiences.

"But now you are free from the power of sin and are slaves of God, and his benefits to you include holiness and everlasting life." [1]

—*Paul to the Romans*

4.

Learning a Servant's Role—in the Valley

During my teens I worked in a home where the wife was a Christian Science reader and practitioner. Since the tenets of her religion clashed with every doctrine which had been implanted within me from childhood and I had no better sense than to ardently defend what I believed, we had some rather lively discussions. While it was all without animosity, it was hardly with benefit.

Perhaps Timothy was also prone to verbal combat, for Paul reminded him, "The servant of the Lord must not strive; but be gentle unto all men, apt to teach, patient. In meekness instructing those that oppose themselves; if God peradventure will give them repentance to the acknowledging of the truth." [2]

Back then, I had little comprehension of the indispensible ministry of the Holy Spirit in bringing to spiritual birth an individual into the family of God. Now I know that an unbeliever doesn't come into a personal relationship with Jesus Christ because someone thought to enlighten him or her by arguing doctrine.

As I remember, one of our most frequent discussions involved whether or not heaven and hell were literal places as the Bible describes them. She defended her viewpoint that they were not by quoting Jesus when He said, "The kingdom of God is within you," [3] and "Repent: for the kingdom of heaven is at hand." [4]

Frankly, I hadn't the vaguest idea what those verses really meant so I shifted over them and pointed to the many graphic descriptions of heaven and hell in the Bible. After all, she was challenging basic Bible truths, and I was out to set her straight. What a lot I had to learn!

Many years passed before I began to glean even a smattering of what Jesus was really saying here. Certainly the human mind cannot begin to comprehend all that the Bible teaches concerning Christ's Kingdom. But as I studied and the Spirit gave light, I became more and more intrigued. How could I have grown up in churches of the Holiness movement, attended other churches too, without even knowing the Kingdom of God was the intrinsic message of the Gospel Jesus preached? I felt I'd been cheated! For I soon realized a whole lifetime of study could never exhaust all that Scripture expounded concerning Christ's Kingdom.

And what was all important, it was to be the here-and-now realm-of-living for the church, and that included me!

I found the verses I had shrugged off in those long ago discussions didn't disprove the reality of heaven and hell. But they underscored the truth that though infinite in scope, the conception of Christ's Kingdom, as it is established on earth, takes place within those who embrace the Lordship of Jesus Christ. And it is manifest in the consecrated obedience of the servants of the King.

I wasn't holding a title deed for a "mansion in the sky," with no further involvement until I stepped through a door marked, "Death." Involvement began the very moment I said, "Lord, I believe," and meant it. True obedience of faith becomes action; I was responsible for becoming involved *now*.

However—it had to be faced—I couldn't become totally involved at *my* level. There was only one way—by letting the Lord cast me in a servant's role. That meant letting Him deal with all that would withstand His absolute control. Such dealings would be and have been painful, but so necessary.

Although as far back as I can remember, I had a hunger for God, I was one who had absorbed the atmosphere and thought myself spiritual. I'd even managed to impress others. Then something happened which precipitated genuine fulfillment of that desire.

One night, unable to sleep, I wandered out to the kitchen. My Bible was lying on the freezer. Indifferently, I flipped it open and began to read: "This people draw near me with their mouth, and with their lips do honour me, but have removed their heart far from me, and their fear toward me is taught by the precept of men." [5] Well that wasn't for me; those Jews in the Old Testament were always acting like that! So I turned to the New . . .

Would you believe it? Here was Matthew quoting Isaiah: "This people . . . honoureth me with their lips; but their heart is far from me. But in vain they do worship me, teaching for doctrines the commandments of men." [6]

Though I wasn't "promise hunting," by now I was thinking there should be something for me. I tried again, this time Mark. Again I read, "This people honoureth me with their lips, but their heart is far from me. Howbeit in vain do they worship me, teaching for doctrines the commandments of men." [7]

In one shattering moment, something deep within my understanding broke, and I saw exactly how it had been. I could only drop to the floor, sobbing out my heart to God.

Though it happened over a dozen years ago, I remember so well how "exposed" I felt that night. It was the beginning of God seeking to reveal myself to me! As the sham and hypocrisy began to be uncovered, I was sick at what I saw. I realized even the doctrines I contended for religiously were not really mine, revealed by the Spirit. They were from men. And doing the "right" things and avoiding the "wrong," was motivated by fear of God instilled by man, not out of love nor my own convictions born of God.

There is no wider expanse than that which separates the religious pharisee and the true servant of God. I was a zealot, defiantly religious, but religion doesn't produce servants, and the Kingdom of God is comprised of servants. It took God's dealings through ex-

treme measures over a long period of time before I was ready to
face many things without defense and accept the discipline of submission. But that night was a new beginning.

Before God can build His Kingdom within us, He must deliver
us from the strong independent human spirit which rebels at submission. Gritting our teeth won't accomplish deliverance; only God
can change our attitude so that our actions come into line with His
will. Our part is to confess our need and be willing for Him to
make us willing to serve at any level.

David's joy in preparing for the building of a house for his God
was contagious. He asked: "Who then is *willing* to consecrate his
service this day unto the Lord?" The response was tremendous:
"Then the people rejoiced, for that they offered *willingly*, because
with perfect heart they offered *willingly* to the Lord," causing David's heart to well up with thanksgiving: "But who am I, and what is
my people, that we should be able to offer so *willingly* after this
sort?" [8]

My father likewise never saw Christian living as an obligation to
be fulfilled grudgingly. He taught me by example to thank the Lord
for the privilege of serving Him.

However, the privilege cannot be enjoyed until there are certain
moral adjustments. Service which is acceptable to the Lord has certain characteristics. And God uses the valleys to effect these necessary adjustments and develop these characteristics.

Merely calling ourselves servants doesn't establish the fact. Each
of God's chosen leaders were recognized by God Himself as the
"servant of the Lord." It was so of Abraham, Jacob, Moses, Caleb,
Joshua, David, Job, Isaiah . . .

All my talk won't make it so; I can be a servant only by serving.
Neither is the service stereotyped; I have no prerogative as to where
it takes me or what it entails. I am only to be concerned that there
is unquestionable obedience and service out of love.

The true servant has several distinguishing marks, though none stand alone, each overlapping. Here is a checklist of those often referred to in Scripture. I don't find it soothing.

1. Filled with the Spirit.
2. Fully obedient.
3. Service by choice.
4. Total commitment out of love.
5. Total identification with the Lord in His humility.
6. Undivided loyalty.
7. No thought for the physical life—even in persecution unto death.
8. Absolute trust that the Lord provides the spiritual, physical, and material needs of His servants.
9. He will receive honor of the Father.

The first two characteristics marked the rewarding difference between Caleb and his brethren who never got into Canaan. The Lord said, "He had another spirit with him, and hath followed me fully." [9]

Paul was another whose life was controlled and anointed by the Holy Spirit. Because he knew his authority in God and that the Spirit was operating through him, Paul dared, in the midst of the storm, to give directions to the commanding officer. But he never forgot he was also a servant of men. Though he was a hero by the time he reached the island of Melita, he stooped to gather sticks with the rest; as a servant he was bitten by the snake.

The Holy Spirit and obedience will always mark those whose service is pleasing to God. What we do on our own apart from the Spirit will remain just that.

No action takes precedence over obedience. Jesus plainly says that it isn't your doctrine or theology which, if correct, gives you the privilege of calling Him Lord. The only one who has the right to address Jesus as Lord is the obedient servant. "Why do you call me Lord, Lord, and not do what I tell you?"

Supernatural manifestations can never substitute for obedience. The Bible is emphatic: "His servants ye are to whom ye obey." [10] To those who would seek to enter the Kingdom for having wrought miracles in the name of Jesus, He will say, "I never knew you!" [11] I wasn't with you: you acted on your own. He alone shall enter in "that doeth the will of my Father which is in heaven." [12]

We pray to be like Jesus, but in what way? Loving, gracious, kind, and good? Or beaten, broken, forsaken, misunderstood, spat upon—without retaliation ever?

Jesus was no do-gooder or miracle worker. He was committed to do the Father's will. He did what He did only as it was revealed to Him by His Father. And He did nothing apart from His Father.

That is why, though there were scores of sick at the pool of Bethesda, Jesus could walk in among them, heal only one, and walk out. That is why he refused to turn the stones into bread, but turned the water into wine. Of Jesus, God had said through the prophet Isaiah, "Behold my servant, whom I uphold; mine elect, in whom my soul delighteth." [13]

A servant is under orders. His job is to obey!

Only in the valley experiences does our obedience to the whole will of God meet the most crucial test. We read, "In every thing give thanks; for this is the will of God in Christ Jesus concerning you." [14] But don't think this just involves minding our spiritual manners and saying, "Thanks." It is living our faith, and by that expressing confidence that everything which God permits is best for us.

Jesus came determinedly doing the Father's will. He totally believed in the Father. It was not healing the blind, delivering the demon-possessed, not even raising Lazarus from the dead which was the greatest act of faith Jesus ever did. It was when, on the night He was betrayed, our Lord, knowing full well what the next hours held, looked up into the face of His Father and gave thanks! At that moment He gave testimony to perfect trust and total submission to the Father's will.

We can't really know if we accept circumstances when we're on the outside looking in. To give thanks when the pressure is on is the true test, and one we face continually. There must be that recognition of His authority that acknowledges in the most difficult valleys, "All the paths of the Lord are mercy." [15] Any other attitude is rebellion.

Obedience demands we give ourselves exclusively to God, not to a calling nor a creed, not rationalizing our will and our rights.

A friend almost ready to take his bar examination when he was converted told me: "I said, 'Lord, I submit my life to You. I'll be a Christian lawyer.' But God said, 'I don't want Christian lawyers, doctors, ministers, or laymen. I want men—yielded to me.' This didn't mean He wouldn't have Christian lawyers, doctors, ministers, and laymen. But my commitment was to be to Christ, not to a profession, whatever it might be." A lawyer first, he later became a missionary, and is now in translation work.

Someone has said, "If man can make a total surrender of self to live completely for self, then indwelt by the power of the Holy Spirit, surely he can make a total surrender of self to God and live completely for Him." Only the power of the Holy Spirit indwelling the life can make this real, but He will, if we let Him. And we must, if we would be His servants.

Service by choice and total commitment out of love, are marks of the Lord's servants, graphically illustrated by the laws concerning Israel's slaves. Six years of service entitled a Hebrew slave to be set free. However, he could choose to remain a servant: "If the servant shall plainly say, I love my master, my wife and my children; I will not go out free." [16] Then he submitted himself to having his ear bored through with an awl, and was thereby committed to serving his master forever. His committal of love to serve had not been without pain.

Midst suffering and persecution can we say, "Mark me, Lord, as one who serves You for love and love alone, not for future reward —except as I see eternity with Thee. What I do, I do for Jesus' sake"?

When the hurricane strikes, the only thing which will ever hold us to this commitment is love. If what we do is for Jesus' sake, we will know His sufficiency and be filled with a spirit of expectancy as to how the Lord will bring us through—rather than how He will spare us the gale. Praise, which is the projection of love, keeps us conscious of His presence as we ride out the storm.

The fifth mark, total identity with the Lord in His humility, will change our direction as nothing else.

Jesus said, "I am meek and lowly in heart." [17] And Paul says, "Let this mind be in you, which was also in Christ Jesus." [18]

What is the mind of Christ? It is that disposition of humility which caused Jesus to empty Himself of every divine prerogative which was His as the Son of God.

From the highest position of all, He assumed the lowest. He bore the stamp of humility from the moment of birth—swaddling clothes and a manger. While He would never be anything less than 100 percent God, at the same time, He became 100 percent man. And as man He became a servant, His time and energy expended to meet humanity's desperate needs. No ministry was beneath Him; Jesus never waited for anyone to wash His feet. Rather we see Him stepping down to the most menial tasks . . . down, down, down . . . giving Himself . . . until He reached the bottom step—death on the Cross.

Jesus plainly shows us the steps down into this valley. He challenges us: "If any man serve me, let him follow me; and where I am, there shall also my servant be." [19]

Several times I have known college students to be called home midterm because they were needed in a crisis. When God indicates that such responsibility is to be accepted for a time, learning suddenly switches from the classroom to the sickroom, to the kitchen, or a job. The right to live independently has come up against the Cross.

To *"let* this mind be in you" is a matter of choice. As the Son of God set aside every divine right which was His and embraced death on the Cross, so must we willingly surrender our rights to be our own masters—if we would be His servants. To take up the Cross is to live sacrificially in every area of our lives.

There must be the sixth mark, that of undivided loyalty, for "No man can serve two masters: for either he will hate the one, and love the other; or else he will hold to the one, and despise the other. Ye cannot serve God and mammon." [20] To try, is to end up frustrated and confused.

Before we come to Christ, most of us are committed twenty-four hours a day to doing what *we* want. But afterward, we lack the same drive to satisfy the heart of God. All too often we still want what we want. James calls it double-mindedness, and we need to be delivered, for uncertainty doesn't beget faith, it engenders spiritual schizophrenia.

If ever a man exhibited the ultimate devotion to an earthly king, it was Ittai, servant of King David. One wonders how he came to such loyalty in the short time he had been captive.

Absalom's devious plot to wrest the kingdom from his father caused David to plan to flee Jerusalem immediately with his servants. Seeing Ittai preparing to accompany them, and knowing both his own and his servants' lives would be in danger, he encouraged Ittai to return with his brethren to his own people.

Ittai's answer is a classic: "As the Lord liveth, and as my lord the king liveth, surely in what place my lord the king shall be, whether in death or life, even there also will thy servant be." [21]

Such was the vow of loyalty spoken by a true servant to his lord. Dare our commitment to the King of kings be less than Ittai's commitment to King David?

It is so easy to shrink from the seventh mark, taking no thought for our life even in persecution, unless we also bear the eighth mark: absolute trust that He provides the spiritual, physical, and material needs of His servants.

Jesus warned, "The servant is not greater than his lord. If they have persecuted me, they will also persecute you." [22]

David's enemies were many. He knew much persecution. But he saw God's hand even in that which caused him much distress. For he said, "It is good for me that I have been afflicted; that I might learn thy statutes." [23]

Stepping out in faith to live by Christ's admonition, "Take no thought for your life," [24] we will be as one who walks the plank, unless we see the deep basic truth which Jesus presented as the bridge to security.

I discovered how power-packed this principle is during another period of pain-racked days and nights. I lay in bed unable to sleep, thinking, "I get so fed up with all the pain and problems it causes; how easy to give up the struggle. Death would be such an easy way out."

Immediately the Lord spoke in a flashback of memories. All too often there had been that disposition to escape life when I was pressed into a difficult place.

And then, in my mind, underlined in red as they were in my Bible, I saw the words, "Take no thought for your life." A whole new sense of their meaning began to break through, which I felt compelled to write down.

But that would mean getting up and going out into the living room. Since everyone else was sleeping, I couldn't use my typewriter. Longhand is very tiring for me. Besides, I hurt from head to toe. I'd had a rough day, had awakened very early that morning from pain—I definitely needed rest! But the Lord wasn't listening to my excuses.

"Let me think about it a little longer; I'll try to write it tomorrow . . ." But I heard, "I thought you were committed to draw from My Spirit. If so, you don't need time to think this through. Just write what I'm showing you—tonight." (All that the Spirit gives doesn't come in this way; more often it is just plain hard work and discipline, writing and rewriting. It can even come through an editor's blue pencil.)

Still reluctant to get up, but afraid of losing the thoughts before morning, I began to realize I had better obey. Later, I understood He was using my own hesitancy as an object lesson, showing me the relationship of my reaction to what He was trying to get through to me. If the Lord said, "Get up and write," and I said, "I'm too tired, I'll do it in the morning," I was obviously taking immediate thought for my life, for my comfort.

When I obeyed, I began to see something far beyond what I had ever seen in that passage before. It wasn't just being unconcerned with material needs because only eternal values are important, and being willing to wear out for Christ, even to becoming a martyr. Jesus was saying much more.

Consider first that Jesus is making a comparison between man's inadequacy and God's all-sufficiency. He contrasts Solomon arrayed in all his splendor—apparel woven by man—as tawdy in appearance beside the lilies of the field—God's handiwork.

Some would try to fashion their own garments to cover sin. But in view of the robe of righteousness which Christ provides for those who come to Him with nothing but a believing and repentant heart, such works are nothing but filthy tattered rags.

"You have sought to follow Me," the Lord said. "It has left you stripped financially. You've been bemoaning what you do not have, that there is so little left. But, so what! Life is more than material things, and the body more than raiment."

Yes, I knew that. But He hadn't finished.

"I have said, 'Take no thought for your life,' because I have a perfect plan for it—foreordained before the foundation of the world. It is that you should know the mystery of God which is: 'Christ in you, the hope of Glory.' Total identity with Me will take care of everything. It is no true servant of Mine whose attitude is: 'I'll do it if it kills me!' "

I began to see. When I take no thought for my life—by faith I hand it over to Jesus and accept a servant's role in order to become a love slave—from then on as His servant I am His responsibility!

What a narrow view I had held of Christ's promise of provision.

It amounted to, "Get saved, and the Lord will see you don't go hungry or without clothes to wear"—well, just about that.

We have known the miraculous provision of God for the material needs of our family, even in small ways. Once when there was no money to buy my husband much-needed socks, I mentioned it quite casually to the Lord. When we came home from church the next Sunday night, seven pairs of socks (God's number of completion) lay just off the sidewalk curb in front of our house. More astounding, those socks wore for years; others had lasted him only a few weeks.

Another time, when my husband was out of work in the winter, and I was pregnant and needed fruit, a box of hand-wrapped Golden Delicious apples spilled off a truck right in front of our house. When my husband hurried out to help pick them up, the driver said, "If you can use them, you can have them," jumped into his truck and sped off. We didn't have much else, but we had the finest apples.

Even so, what God is saying here is so much more involved than apples or socks. There are needs other than physical ones.

I remember when I had to send our oldest son off to school without lunch money; yet we were in a Christian training school and trusting the Lord's promise to provide all our needs. We had known His supply so many times! What was wrong now?

Nothing! God was supplying the greater need.

He knew the greatest need I had was to know Jesus as Lord in experience, not just in theory. Theory, I learned in the classroom. Theory and theology became experience when I sat down to lunch that noon, thinking about not having anything to send with my son for lunch at public school.

We simply cannot escape the claims of His Lordship in the here-and-now action of day-in-and-day-out life. But seeking out the Kingdom of God and His righteousness—letting Him build His Kingdom within—leaves nothing lacking.

While our life becomes relatively unimportant when we have the flow of His life within, at the same time, there will be the full expression of life involving our whole person. The life of the resurrected Christ is the veritable source of "all these things" which He has promised.

What are "all these things" which are supplied to His servants?

Surely they include the necessities of today, because Jesus doesn't write them off as not being needful. But He places the emphasis on the fact that these are transient—food, raiment, the length of one's days. In other words, what most people consider life isn't life at all. The Father sees into the heart and into the eternities, and He alone knows what is the real need.

So He says, "Make Me Lord of your life—seek the Kingdom and the righteousness of God. Then you will have discovered the ultimate. Take up your Cross and follow Me, 'for whosoever will save his life shall lose it; but whosoever shall lose his life for my sake and the gospel's, the same shall save it!' " [25]

Life—not physical energy, but that personality which we are, timeless, eternal in existence, God's gift that we might share the Trinity Love, both in the moment in which we live and throughout the eternity of eternities.

Life for the Christian is relationship and communion with God, fellowship with the brethren, God's love flowing in and through in ministry to the unbeliever. Life is what we do during the twenty-four hours of the day. It applies to our total existence as we know it on this earth. Life in Christ is as eternal as God Himself.

And so "all things" does not just bracket material needs supplied and eternal reward. Jesus Christ provides every resource I need to live "to the praise of his glory." [26]

I know that when my obedience is full, I shall bear the ninth mark, recognition by my Father. For Jesus said, "If any man serve me, let him follow me; . . . if any man serve me, him will my Father honour." [27] Recognition shall come through an outflow ministry marked by His blessing and confirmed by Him.

God wants us to know the miraculous, since the supernatural power of God is to be a means, a part of our outflow ministry. That which matures and stabilizes us in God, enabling us to stand unde-feated in battle, however, doesn't come from a display of the mirac-ulous, but obedience. Obedience produces the proper conditions for God to make known His presence in the midst of His people by signs and wonders.

Total submission in every circumstance automatically makes us revolutionaries: we cross a battle line few have stepped across. Pure and unparalleled romance of life is in this oft unexplored territory. For nothing could be more completely contrary to popular concept than for submission to be the detonator of power, especially power which is paramount—the supernatural limitless power of God.

Yet it is that very act of total submission which triggers the ex-plosive power of the Spirit, and immediately involves us in the most relevant, the most urgent, the most timely of all causes—the full ushering in of the Kingdom of Jesus Christ. Our heritage in the Kingdom depends upon our total submission to the King.

For years I had claimed Isaiah 54:13,17: "All thy children shall be taught of the Lord. . . . This is the heritage of the servants of the Lord." But one day the Lord spotlighted that word "servants." If I claimed the promise, I had to accept the condition—the position of "servant of the Lord."

Much of the struggle against submission comes out of fear. We are afraid of being taken advantage of; afraid of not getting our own way; afraid we won't be treated as we think we deserve; afraid that when we are hurt, we won't be able to voice our true feelings; afraid we won't get what we feel should be coming to us.

True, a servant has no rights. But in submission there is security and complete provision for those who have learned total depen-dence upon God.

The choice of accepting a servant's role comes to each of us indi-vidually. When we have made that choice of commitment, there is only this one direction. After Jesus stooped down to wash the disci-ples' feet, He said: "I have given you an example, that ye should do as I have done to you. . . . The servant is not greater than his lord." [28]

If we follow that example, we will be led down a long flight of steps, down into the valleys; down to where, if He is absolute Lord, we have no rights . . . where there is death to self's assertion . . . where there is only the Cross . . . down . . .

But it is such submission in the most formidable valleys that produces the ultimate of faith and vision. Here we learn to appropriate the full provision of the King. There is no lack in Him! And neither moments of ecstasy, riches, poverty, health, sickness, nor crushing blows determine our relationship to Jesus Christ, nor in themselves vary it.

Only when the Lord can call us His obedient servants, will we know that security whereby we can walk with dauntless courage into every stronghold of the enemy, untormented in spirit and unshaken in faith. And the dividends will be beyond what we can imagine.

He will be able to call us his obedient servants if, when we hear His voice, we have but one answer to His orders: "Yes, Lord!"

"He who covers and forgives an offense seeks love, but he who repeats or harps on a matter separates even close friends." [1]

—*Solomon*

5.

Learning Love—in the Valley

Yes, I know what it is to be hurt so deeply that human love fails; I've been there where I had nothing to give. But I made a discovery. The Lord wasn't asking me to minister human love; He was asking me to minister His love. And the Lord took me into a valley of untold heartache to teach me the difference.

Because I had been hurt so deeply, I began to build a mental and emotional barrier, a thick shell. And I began to put limits on my love. In some areas I refused to love. I had been hurt; I didn't intend to get hurt again.

Hardly before I realized it, the barrier became so strong that even when I wanted to, I couldn't break through. In some relationships, there wasn't the least desire to break through, I was so scared of getting hurt. Yet by temperament, loving comes easily to me, so I was really at conflict with myself.

You can't go through such a struggle without it affecting you mentally, emotionally, and physically, as well as making you spiritually incapacitated. God never withdrew any of the pressure until I fully understood the cause and effect, until I realized that I was stubbornly refusing to let God break me or break through the barrier.

Our doctor, friend of the family, talked with me about the hurt, the emotional upheaval, the scarring.

"I've been hurt so deeply, I'm afraid to love for fear of being hurt again." I was defensive.

I shall never forget his answer: "But that is the cost of love! You are going to love—and you are going to get hurt again. Look at what God's love cost Him!"

The cost of love . . . I couldn't get away from the thought. It wasn't the one who had caused the hurts that was my problem, it was me. I hadn't wanted to love for fear it would cost more heartache. I had rebelled against God's command to love, and so I was still locked inside the shell I'd built. I didn't have the power within myself to break free, but I did begin to pray that God would do what I couldn't do.

I knew it would take the supernatural. "Lord, make me willing to love—no matter if it deepens the hurts that are already there. Whatever it takes, I want my will parallel to God's will, not cutting across it or fighting against it."

God didn't remove the barrier in one mighty swoop, but He began by cracking the wall in an unusual happening.

During a week of meetings being held some distance from our home, I became increasingly conscious of my need for deliverance. One evening after the service, I walked into another building where a young man stood leaning against the wall. I saw at once he was high on dope. A young minister who worked with hippies was trying to talk to him; two other couples stood close by.

I had hardly walked through the door, and at a glance taken in what was happening at the other end of the room, before the Lord clearly said, "Ask that boy how old he is. If he is the same age as one of your sons, go put your arms around him and give him a mother's kiss and a mother's love." I nearly froze in my tracks!

"But, Lord! I don't even *like* hippies."

Besides, I'd never been that close to anyone as high as he was. Then I began to figure: I have a boy almost seventeen, one eighteen, and one twenty-one—he looks perhaps twenty-two. But maybe he'll fall between their ages . . .

All the while, I was so compelled by the Lord's voice it was frightening. I took a few steps closer, where I could hear what was being said. I could see by the boy's reaction, how befuddled his mind was, and even though he was being spoken to in wisdom and love, that it wasn't getting through.

The Lord prodded me hard: "NOW!" I was scared to obey— more scared not to obey. Heart pounding, I took a deep breath and then that first step.

"Son," I said gently, "how old are you?"

He looked at me wearily. "Eighteen."

My eighteen-year-old had left home the week before; the empty ache was still there.

I reached up and put a hand on each of his shoulders and said, "Son—I have a boy eighteen. I want to give you a mother's kiss as a friend of God." By then the tears were flowing; I couldn't stop them—and God had His chisel in the barrier I had erected and refused for so long to let Him break through.

Suddenly, I began to feel the flow of God's love through me, my arms went around the boy, and it was as if I was holding my own son. His cheek against mine burned with fever, our tears mingled. I went on: "As God, the Father, loved His Son, and Jesus has given His love to me, I want to give His love to you. Know that He loves you so much!"

I believe God put every word in my mouth during the next half-hour. I knew nothing of the boy's background, nor did I even know those who had been talking with him. Yet they sensed that God was doing something, and they graciously stepped back. Never had I felt the force of the flow of God's love to anyone as I did to that boy.

I discovered that he did not know the identity of his natural parents, that he had been given away at birth, had been on the road since eleven, on drugs since fourteen. I said, "It has always bothered you because you haven't known who you were, hasn't it?"

He only held me more fiercely, and I could feel the deep hurting sobs. I stepped back enough so that I could look directly into his eyes, and I called him by name. I said, "If you never remember anything else I say to you tonight, don't ever forget this: You were born right out of the very heart of God's love! So you do have a Father—God, Himself! And I want to be a mother to you by praying for you just as if you were my own son, so now you do have a mother. God is your Father, and He loves you!"

Had I planned what I was going to say, I don't know as I'd have put it this way at all. Knowing me, I'd have questioned whether such statements were orthodox. Some would debate the issue.

But the Spirit of God was working two ways—in me and in him. And I was conscious only that God's love was flowing like a river, breaking me, breaking the barrier, bringing clarity to that boy's mind. While we talked, I saw his understanding return, and when I kissed him goodnight and left, the minister was able to step to his side to take him to his room for further prayer.

The next day when I saw the boy, his long hair was cut, and one would never have guessed his condition the night before.

What that experience meant to him in the months following, I've no way of knowing. I pray for him and shall continue to do so. But I know what it did for me! If anyone had told me that God would use a hippie to break through my shell, to start love flowing in me again, I wouldn't have believed it. But that is exactly what God did. And I've never felt quite the same about hippies since.

When I took the first step of obedience, I learned something new and precious about the outflow of God's love. That night wasn't a point of arrival, but it was definitely a point of beginning.

Yes, in my life there have been struggles to love, even since then. But there has also been a drastic change within. More and more I realize the cost of love. And that when there is nothing of human love from which to draw, I can simply say, "Lord, I can't give love which I don't have. But as I submit to You, I can give Your love." So I can affirm my love without hypocrisy.

I have also been learning to appropriate the love of God through the flow of the Spirit—and to release that love to others.

My mother taught me, by her unselfish example, how love meets practical issues.

Mother's affection for Dad wasn't often demonstrated by hugs and kisses.

"Why don't you ever show Dad that you love him?" I asked her once.

It was during World War II, a time when farmers found it almost impossible to get reliable help. Dad owned purebred cattle; he couldn't let just anyone milk his test herd, for a neglected milking machine could ruin a prize cow in a matter of minutes. Mother got up before five those dark winter mornings to help run the machines. What's more, she did it cheerfully.

"Show him I love him?" Mother gave me one of her famous exasperated looks. "Don't you think that when I crawl out of bed at 4:30 in the morning to go to the barn, I'm showing him love more than if I was always going around hugging and kissing him and saying a lot of lovey-dovey words?"

Of course, I knew my mother loved my father. But kid that I was, I wanted a sentimental demonstration.

I still think my idea was a good one. But Mother's love went much deeper than mere sentiment. She understood, far better than I did then, that love is much more than a sentimental feeling.

One doesn't embrace Jesus Christ as Lord—regardless—without soon discovering that the acid test of that commitment is to love—regardless. In fact, in every spiritual battle, at some point, we will be challenged as to the divine quality of our love.

Jesus gives us a three-point outline of action to follow when love is tested: the word of action, the deed of action, and the action of the Spirit.

He said, "Bless them that curse you." [2] This is the word of action. When someone curses you, your immediate response is to be a word of blessing!

Someone told me of a friend, witnessing in the skid-row section of a large city, being attacked by a gang of ruffians. As they ran off, leaving him lying in the dust where their blows had felled him, he raised his hand and called to them, "The Lord bless you!"

Could any action be more shattering to the offenders?

Under such circumstances, you might feel spiritually elated if you managed to keep your mouth shut and not scream at your assailants. And for most of us, keeping still would be a victory. But the Lord wants us to be more than conquerors over that enemy sniper, the tongue. It is to be under complete submission to the King. It is to "bless, and curse not."

"Do good to them that hate you." [3] This is the deed of action.

Since hate, too, is an action word, Jesus' command evidently refers specifically to those who have openly shown evil feelings toward us.

Some years ago, I came across this remarkable account of one man's obedience.

During the Revolutionary War, word came to the pastor of a church in Pennsylvania that a certain man had been sentenced to death for treason. Though the traitor had caused untold trouble for Pastor Miller and the members of his church, he at once started out on foot to intercede for the man's life. He appealed to General Washington himself.

"I'm sorry," was the general's reply. "This man is guilty. I cannot spare your friend's life."

"Friend?" the pastor exclaimed. "Why, I haven't a worse enemy living than that man!"

"What! You walked sixty miles to save the life of an enemy? Well, I would say that puts the whole thing in a different light."

With a pardon in his hand, the old pastor hurried on to the place of execution. He had covered the fifteen miles just as the man was being led to the scaffold.

The condemned man, seeing the pastor he had so terribly wronged, muttered, "So Pastor Miller has come all the way to have his revenge gratified by seeing me hanged."

Pastor Miller answered by putting in the man's hand the pardon which spared his life.

Though you are not likely to find yourself involved in such a dramatic situation, you are bound to encounter, from day to day, those who "hate" you.

Jesus does not tell us to ignore such people, neither are we merely to think kindly of them. Rather, we are deliberately to follow a course of action that will help the person who has injured us. Such conduct on our part will have a potent effect. We will find ourselves caring for the person for whom we have done something.

"Pray for them which despitefully use you." [4] This is the action of the Spirit.

Apart from the Holy Spirit, this kind of prayer would be an impossibility. Such intercession involves a deliberate act, a choice we make—the choice to pray. This choice results in a transformation of our inner self, for the Spirit which flows through us in prayer, also flows through us in love to change our attitude toward that person.

So often, we try to sandpaper our experience or plane a little off the sharp edge of God's truth as plainly stated in the Word, to make our experience or lack of experience conform to His Truth. Believe me, it doesn't work. All I ever got for the effort was a conscience full of splinters.

I couldn't get around the commandment to love. But knowing that love was more than sentiment, that it involved action, I decided that I was responsible only for my actions. I argued that I couldn't feel what I didn't feel. So if I "did good" to the one who had hurt me or the one toward whom I didn't feel love, God would be satisfied; I wasn't responsible for my attitude. But it worked only to a degree.

One day I opened my *Amplified New Testament* and read: "Love endures long and is patient and kind; love never is envious nor boils over with jealousy; is not boastful or vainglorious, does not display itself haughtily. It is not conceited—arrogant and inflated with pride; it is not rude (unmannerly), and does not act unbecomingly. Love [God's love in us] does not insist on its own rights or its own way, for it is not self-seeking; it is not touchy or fretful or resentful; it takes no account of the evil done to it—pays no attention to a suffered wrong. It does not rejoice at injustice and unrighteousness, but rejoices when right and truth prevail. Love bears up under anything and everything that comes, is ever ready to believe the best of every person, its hopes are fadeless under all circumstances and it endures everything." [5]

How could I have held I was not responsible for an *attitude* lacking the disposition of God's love!

The Lord held me to the line until I was forced to admit that God's love was action *and* attitude. To love as Jesus commanded, I must put my attitude under His control; for I know that by sheer determination of will, man can act and react in the very best interest of another, and yet know nothing of the innate source of divine love.

Feelings are mercurial, but attitude is a disposition of the will. God has made provision that our attitude, actions, and reactions may line up with His command—regardless of our feelings.

First, however, we must admit to any unloving attitudes for which we have made allowances, thinking certain individuals don't deserve our love. As long as we hold on to these attitudes, daring to justify them, we can't expect to know God's love flowing in and through.

Communion with God—worship, adoration, praise—is love expressed independently of all other relationships. However, we will soon find there's a breakdown in our communion and communication with the Lord if there's a break in communication with a brother for which we are in any way to blame.

Worship of a Holy God is impossible while resentment, bitterness, or ill will rankle deep within, undealt with, unconfessed and uncleansed; or if we have failed to do everything possible to make things right with the one whom we have offended.

Spiritual hypocrisy is most glaringly exposed in our family relationships. When I read the account of a father who shouted at his teenage son for interrupting his "devotions," I was sure it wasn't only the son who wrote them off as phony.

Whatever the action required to love, I can't do it myself. Inside the church or outside of it, I must know my resource in God.

To understand the provision, consider that love to God and love to man run as an unbroken cord throughout the entire Bible. Jesus said that "all the other commandments and all the demands of the prophets stem from these two laws and are fulfilled if you obey them." [6] His ministry dealt much with man's love to God and to his fellowman; the obligation so to love is built into the whole structure of the Kingdom of God.

That is why it used to seem strange to me, that after Jesus had eaten the last supper with His disciples and Judas had left the room, Jesus made the statement, "A new commandment I give unto you, That ye love one another; as I have loved you, that ye also love one another." [7]

The word "new" puzzled me! What could go beyond the demands of love already set forth by Jesus in Luke 6:27–38? Surely, He had gone the limit there!

The commandment of love was not new; therefore, He could be speaking only of a new dimension or quality of love.

But what would be the intrinsic nature of such love? What would be the essentials? I had to know if I were to keep this "new" commandment.

The first clue, I found in the first verse of that same chapter: "Having loved His own . . . He loved them unto the end." [8]

God is Love. God is eternal. Therefore, God's love is eternal. God's love will have an eternal quality which does not fluctuate according to what the other person does, or is, or does not do. If it is God's love, it will remain steadfast because of who God is.

But all this will be only so much theory until we discover that the new quality of our love must come out of a new relationship and our becoming established in that relationship until it becomes the most dominant factor in our life.

Jesus prayed for the church as He saw it in existence throughout succeeding generations. "I in them, and thou in me, that they may be made perfect in one; and that the world may know that thou hast sent me, and hast loved them, as thou hast loved me . . . that the love wherewith thou hast loved me may be in them, and I in them." [9]

That we can know this oneness with the Father and Son—a provision which springs from the heart of God—Paul says, is the "mystery of godliness."

How can we read the 17th chapter of John and yet at times go around as if we didn't know who we are nor where we are going, acting as though somehow we'd been lost in the shuffle? Our position in Christ was secured, sealed when the Father glorified the Son.

But every provision of grace must be received through faith. Submission to Jesus as Lord releases faith to appropriate this mystery: "Christ in you, the hope of glory" [10] becomes reality.

When Jesus prayed, "I in them and thou in me . . ." He was talking about both an established position and a definite relationship. Herein is the assurance that I can live in victory, for all things are under His feet and I am in Him. Because of my union with Jesus Christ, I do have authority over every evil force that would prevent the outworking of the Holy Spirit. And I am indwelt by the very source of love.

However, it is the Spirit of God which releases that love. Until there has been that vertical inflow through the Spirit, it is impossible for me to be a channel for the horizontal outflow of God's love. "The love of God is shed abroad in our hearts by the Holy Ghost which is given unto us." [11] But it isn't just to create "atmosphere." God has given us nine tools of the Spirit to enable us to give substance to our love.

As we learn how to move according to the guidance of the Spirit, we will find divine love is the only key which will unlock the chains which bind many so securely. They will never find release unless there is a personal ministry of the love of God to them in the power of the Holy Spirit. Consequently, we begin to understand that God's love is more than an unmerited favor, a blessing to be enjoyed by "me and mine." To hold the key of deliverance and release into the blessings of the Kingdom for the desolate and desperate, is an awesome responsibility.

God's love is without dissimulation. There can be no man preferred, no man excluded. God's love must spread across the whole spectrum of our relationships or we are perverting that which is holy.

No matter how "lovable" you may seem, the world is quick to discern the touch of condescension. Nothing turns them off faster than condescension, and nothing makes it harder to reach them afterward, even if later they contact the genuine. If you cannot minister life through the reality of God's love abiding within, for His sake, do not through hypocrisy minister death!

Especially if we've always lived a decent moral life or have been deeply religious, we quite likely consider ourselves more worthy of God's love than the obviously depraved character. But whatever our moral or social level, Jesus went through the same agonies of hell for you and me, every bit as much as He did for anyone else.

Once when I was keenly aware that my attitude was one of revulsion for a certain person, and I did not want to love, God held this verse before me: "But God, who is rich in mercy, for his great love wherewith he loved us even when we were dead in sins, hath quickened us together with Christ." [12]

He said, "Compared to My sinless purity, this was your condition. You were nothing more than a dead stinking corpse, yet I died for you. And more, I gave my life also for the one you say you can't love!"

I can't fathom the magnitude of such love! But having loved me so, He asks me to love for His sake.

Many times I've told the Lord, "I can't! I can't love anyone who acts like that." And the answer is always the same: "I didn't ask you to love them for what they are; I asked you to love them for My sake."

Even though our comprehension of such love is limited, our response must be without reservation, not only Godward, nor to the lovable, but to the most unlovable. Jesus was explicit: "If ye love them which love you, what reward have ye? Do not even the publicans the same?" [13]

The rich young ruler who fell at Jesus' feet, imploring, "Good Master, what good thing shall I do, that I may have eternal life?" [14] was challenged by Jesus as to why he had called Him good; only God is good.

Does he understand that he is at the feet of the Son of God? He gives no indication of such insight, though he declares that he has kept the moral laws since his youth. Jesus doesn't dispute his claim. Looking at him, Jesus loved him. The love of God always demands a response though, and here there is a breakdown.

Jesus said, "One thing thou lackest: go thy way, sell whatsoever thou hast, and give to the poor, and thou shalt have treasure in heaven: and come, take up the cross, and follow me." [15]

This young man had scrupulously kept the law, yet he failed the test of unfeigned love. He was in bondage to his riches. Tragically, he never recognized the Lord, submission to whom would have immediately broken the bondage and released the power of God's love; with joy he would have given to the poor, embraced the Cross, and following Jesus would have known an unequated intimate relationship with the King of kings.

Instead he went away sorrowful. And the day would come when

his sorrow would turn to bitter remorse, when he saw that the tinsel to which he had clung had deprived him of all love offered—the exceeding and eternal riches which are in Christ Jesus.

Religious to the nth degree, he had met every claim but one. But it was the one on which his present joy and his eternal destiny pivoted.

Are we, likewise, willing to practice all the "dos" and "don'ts" and yet unwilling to surrender to His working when He says, "I want to bring your love into focus"? Do we freeze someone out when Jesus says to give them His love? Do we see love as a choice, rather than a command?

If Jesus is Lord, we have no choice but to enter into that relationship where the love of God indwells our being and flows out to every man, excluding no one. Jesus never demands the impossible.

You ask, "Do you mean that you like everybody?" No, I'm no different than you. There are some people whose mannerisms, speech, attitudes, and bearing give me the same sensation as the sound of nails being scratched on a blackboard. You know how it is: just being around them sets my teeth on edge. (No doubt there is a turnabout effect.) What about the way I "feel" around them?

Here again, we have to make the distinction between attitude and feeling, and a difference between human love and God's love. It helps to consider Paul's statement, "In lowliness of mind let each esteem other better than themselves . . . Let this mind be in you, which was also in Christ Jesus . . ." [16]

Admittedly, I have looked at some people, and said, "Lord, just *how* do I esteem him better?" And it seemed the Lord's answer was, "I put your good and your eternal destiny before any right I had, even as the Son of God, even to enjoy the good things which I have created. I claimed nothing for Myself, not even My life; I put you before everything!"

He showed me this was "how."

Likewise, this was to be my attitude in contrast to my feelings. Whenever there is a conflict of preferences, I can "esteem my brother better than myself," simply by yielding my preference, being ready always to assume the lowlier position. Not making a big deal of it, but simply putting his desires even before my "rights." To have the mind of Christ is to put others before everything I prefer. Again I am forced to draw on the resources of the Holy Spirit.

On the negative side, criticism will quickly short-circuit God's love flowing in and through.

A classmate in Bible school told me, "One day, the Lord really dealt with me about the critical spirit I had developed. Then I saw how little there was of Christ's love in my heart. I spent a long afternoon in prayer, arguing with myself that I couldn't generate a feeling of love that wasn't there. Finally the Holy Spirit brought light with these words: 'If you will choose not to criticize, I will choose to fill you with the love of Jesus.' It really worked!"

It is becoming more and more real to me, the force of divine love; the most vital force in the universe is God's love. Certainly it is an expulsive force, for John tells us, "Perfect love casteth out all fear." [17]

Once when I desperately needed deliverance from certain fears, I "happened" onto a very old book. As I turned the stiff yellowed pages, I came upon some thoughts which held me captive. The writer pointed out that when Mary and Martha sent word to Jesus that their brother Lazarus was sick, they said, "Lord, behold, he whom thou lovest is sick." And we read, "Now Jesus loved Martha, and her sister, and Lazarus." [18]

Lazarus loved Jesus too. But it was not the imperfect love of Lazarus for the Lord which delivered him from death, but rather the perfect love of Jesus which set him free.

That night as I walked in the darkness and looked up at the midnight sky, I asked the Lord to forgive me for ever asking Him to meet my need for the reason that I loved Him. "From now on," I told Him, "I am trusting Your perfect love." I saw how it was not on the basis of my imperfect love I would know deliverance, but His perfect love which alone would release me from the grave-clothes which had me bound.

I will never forget the moment when it seemed like my whole being was being washed through with His perfect love. Fear and bondage had to go!

I'm discovering that God's love is a force so powerful, it can bridge any distance. Nothing can stop it. God's love can move into a situation at any level to change circumstances and lives, working according to our faith and obedience.

For the river of God's love to flow in and through us to others, the channel must be kept clean, our position and relationship steadfast in Christ. To love for Jesus' sake is the only motivation which will hold up under fire, the only incentive that will outweigh the "cost."

Whatever you discover the cost of love to be—you will find the cost not to love is greater, if for no other reason than that only the person who can both receive and give love freely is a well-balanced individual. Psychologists are well aware of the relation of mental health to the ability to give and receive love.

If you take all the hurts to the One who understands so perfectly —and choose to keep on loving—the power of God's love will be released through you to change the lives of those you touch.

The action of the Spirit will work in you to enable you to love as you would not think possible—in word and deed and attitude. The world will see and know if His love is abiding in you.

"The goodness of God endureth continually." [1]
—*David*

6.

Understanding the Goodness of God

It was on a Sunday morning in the hospital forty-eight hours after the explosion which nearly took my husband's life. I listened to the brain surgeon explaining the extent of Al's injuries. The lab reports had confirmed what had been feared: it *was* spinal fluid dripping from his nose.

"It was a miracle his head wasn't blown clear off," the doctor said. "Somebody up there certainly must have been looking out for him . . ."

Perhaps some thought it was the thing to say, others really did believe it was true, but it was always the same. I was reminded over and over, by those who were Christians and those who were not, how good God was to spare my husband's life.

Sometimes I could hardly refrain from shouting, "No! No! You don't understand! God is good—period! Whether Al lives or dies has nothing to do with God's character. My God is good—regardless. Regardless of anything!"

Of course, I knew it was God's doing and a miracle that Al's life had been spared, and I was very grateful. I needed him; our three boys needed their dad, and there would be another child soon.

But do you know why I reacted so violently within?

That Sunday morning I had been sitting, talking with a girl in

73

the waiting room of the intensive-care unit. Her husband had seemed to be completely recovered from a light case of flu. But he had suddenly blacked out and had been rushed to the hospital.

As soon as the surgeon finished talking with me, he took the young woman by the arm and led her into the consultation room next-door, followed by another doctor and nurse. Within that same hour, that young mother was left a widow with several small children. A blood vessel had burst in her husband's brain; he never regained consciousness.

What do you think would have been your reaction if you had been that girl and I had just said to you, "God was so good to spare my husband's life"?

From our limited conversation, I gathered she had little background of faith from which to draw. Suppose I had told her that my husband's life had been spared because of a miracle—as an answer to prayer—or had emphasized it was because of God's goodness that my husband was alive—and then she had looked at me grimly and said, "But mine died."

What could I possibly have said just then that would have made any sense to her, that would have made her feel anything but cheated and resentful, that would not have made her mad at God? Though our testimony may be sincere, if we relate God's goodness only to blessing according to man's logic, it can have a disastrous effect on another. To one who has no knowledge at all of God's ways to act as a balancing factor, it can turn them farther from God. If we would minister life and not death, in giving witness, our testimony must not distort the truth.

There is a common tendency among Christians to wrongly interpret the goodness of God. Often this shows up in the invitation to follow Christ which is subtly impregnated with false promises. In effect, the non-Christian is offered a sort of two-cars-in-every-garage deal. The implication is that accepting Christ is a sure guarantee of health, wealth, and a happy-ever-after ending to all problems, tragedies being the chief lot of those who reject Him.

But is this telling it like it is? The rain falls on the just and the unjust alike. A sovereign God chooses the precise formula, bitter or sweet, which will nourish the babe in Christ according to the individual need, in order that he will develop into a mature believer.

From what I've observed, real saints of God have gone through the fire. Others, who apparently never give God a second thought, live lives of comparative ease.

It has always been so. David, Job, and others too, had been more than a little baffled to see the suffering of the righteous and the prosperity of the evil. However, though they saw that which made them wonder, they never pretended it was otherwise.

God in Scripture strips everything down to bare facts. And He expects us to read to the world all the fine print. To entice nonbelievers to come to Christ by presenting them with a distorted concept of what the Christian life is all about, is to sell Christianity short. And he who has based his decision on the false assumption that there will be no more headaches, heartaches, or conflicts is headed for a rude awakening. The real battle has just begun. And the law of sowing and reaping will remain as sure in this life and as universal as the law of gravity. Christians have no automatic immunity.

Of course, the connotation of all invitations to come to Christ is not "everything going my way" for the Christian. The emphasis varies. The "fire insurance" salesmen see Christianity only as an escape from hell. Some sell a paid-up policy: after the initial investment there is no more cost. Others indicate by sales pitch and example that the premium demands going through life with a long face, being a pauper, being "peculiar" for the sake of being peculiar, and exhibiting a martyr complex.

There are, no doubt, many reasons why these false impressions are projected, but basically, I believe all are initiated by a dire lack of understanding of the goodness of God.

Adversity may not shake your faith in God; you may accept it without complaint; but do you really apprehend the goodness of God manifest in all things? Even when God's love is expressed in

ways not generally recognized, do you still retain the same quiet
certitude and confident trust?

Because they have never had a revelation of God's love, few
Christians even begin to understand the goodness of God in the
bitter cup they are sometimes forced to drink, and so they are shattered by the experience.

It took just such a breaking for me to realize, for all my religious
background and babble, that I had never really seen God's hand of
love holding "the cup."

Being wife, mother, and student in a strictly regimented missionary training center, I had incessant demands on my time and energy. That God had brought us into this situation, I knew, but the
difficulties which seemed to adversely affect the children and break
family relationships were out of my control. When I saw what was
happening and felt my helplessness to do anything about it, I was
confused and depressed. I felt very akin to David when he said,
"My tears have been my food day and night, while men say to me
all day long, where is your God?" [2]

I began to wonder too.

With that knowing which comes from God, my pastor, the Rev.
T. A. Hegre exposed the real problem.

"You don't really believe God loves you . . ."

My retort left no doubt that I considered this an utterly stupid
accusation: I couldn't remember back to a time when I didn't know
God loved me. But that didn't dissuade Ted Hegre. He persisted;
what I desperately needed was a revelation of God's love, and for
this he was praying. He couldn't have done me a greater favor; he
couldn't have been more right!

Only when there was that divine illumination of God's perfect
love in the breaking experience was I able to accept the difficulties
without fighting back on the inside. And even when I had difficulty
accepting, I no longer saw these things happening as apart from
God's love. From that time on, talking about God's goodness was
no longer religious jargon; I knew God loved me!

The only reason Paul could write, "In every thing give thanks: for this is the will of God in Christ Jesus concerning you," [3] is because he understood the goodness of God. He knew that what others could see only as the worst possible catastrophe could be immeasurable goodness from a God who is perfect love.

Was the faith of John the Baptist, or the goodness of God at the time John baptized Jesus in the Jordan, any greater than five minutes before John's head was chopped off at the order of a drunken, sensual king? The disciples had known miraculous deliverances from prison, but later Paul spent years in chains and Peter was crucified head downward. If you can equate the goodness of God only with the miraculous and with blessing, how are you going to explain the ultimate fate of these two men?

I declare that God is changeless in all His attributes, that Jesus, in order to gain disciples, never projected any false concepts of what it meant to follow Him. He made it very plain; when we turn our lives over to Him, He immediately puts us in the conflict. Jesus never told anyone who followed Him that it would be easy.

Becoming a Christian doesn't mean God answers the buzzer every time you ring for service, that all your problems are immediately ironed out, or that He stands by just waiting to cater to all your whimsical wants.

Becoming a Christian guarantees you only one sure thing to call your own—a Cross to carry—engraved with your name by nail-pierced hands. And it guarantees His promise to supply all your needs.

Sometimes I am nonplussed at the attitude taken by some Christians. They seem to think God will set aside any of the natural laws of the universe whenever or wherever they are concerned.

The tiniest fragment that makes up the totality of all things that exist, is controlled by innate laws of nature. God's purpose in establishing these laws was for man's good. With each step of creation, "God saw that it was good." [4] But nothing which He made could have fulfilled its purpose in the universe had it not been created subject to certain fixed laws. Surely the natural laws which govern His creation fit into a plan and purpose of God that far exceeds our finite vision.

True, God does interrupt these laws on occasion. I knew a missionary whose family had to travel across a burning desert. It would have been unbearable except for a small cloud which hovered over them, giving shade for the entire journey. And of course, there is the biblical account of the sun standing still, and the time no rain fell for three years. But it would create incomprehensible havoc throughout the whole of His creation, if God was always changing gears.

We have often laughed about the time our little daughter spent her first winter in New York state. All she could remember was Arizona's sunshine-in-December, and she wanted snow. So she prayed. And the next day we got snow. In fact, we had a near blizzard. And in the weeks that followed we had more snow and more snow.

Jan was convinced it had all happened in answer to her prayer. One night she finished off her bedtime prayer with "And God, we don't need any more snow. We've had enough!"

If we are going to flow with God, we need to understand that God does not have two creations; we need to understand that everything which He has brought into being is intimately united in expressing His eternal purpose. People break the natural laws with such careless abandon—Christians, often, on the pretext of faith. But true faith accepts everything which God has brought into existence as being for our ultimate good.

God's disciplines in your life will never accomplish what God intends unless you are fully persuaded of the goodness of God. If my love for God is expressed in obedience to the voice of the Spirit, then I know that "all things work together for good" to conform me to the image of Jesus.[5] Therefore I know that whatever comes into my life, God is good—not merely that He can do me no wrong—but that what He does is the best.

Recently I borrowed the book, *The Release of the Spirit*, by

Watchman Nee, from friends, medical missionaries in the States on extended furlough.

Reading through it, I noticed a date penned in the margin alongside some underscored lines. I was immediately caught up by their significance. I read them with tears in my heart.

"Lord, for the future of the church, for the future of the Gospel, for Thy way, and also for my own life, I offer myself without condition, without reservation, into Thy hands. Lord, I delight to offer myself unto Thee and am willing to let Thee have Thy full way through me." [6]

I began to tick off the months on my fingers; I well understood the significance of the date. It could only have been when the doctor and his family were waiting final word as to whether conference finances would be available for them to go back to the people to which they had ministered and whom they had held in their hearts for seventeen years.

But the summer ended, and there were no finances available. And three months after that prayer had been underscored and dated by the doctor, he had undergone radical surgery for cancer. He had offered himself, willingly . . .

God had accepted the offering and touched the sacrifice with fire in the valley of disappointment, in pain and suffering. But I watched when it happened, and there was no straining at the ropes which bound the sacrifice to the altar. To many who stood by, watching, praying, the tremendous peace and total lack of anxiety was in itself nothing less than a miracle. There was no doubt in anyone's mind that the doctor had absolute confidence in the goodness of God. Therefore, he could relax and let God be God.

I have always considered that one of the greatest personal gifts of God to me has been the privilege of calling Harold J. Brokke, pastor, teacher, friend. What he taught me, by his life and from God's Word, have been priceless, deep truths that have changed my life.

It was his wife, Cathy, who brought me the news at the time my husband was injured. And during the weeks Al was in the hospital, it was to Harold and Cathy we both turned most quickly in our hurt. It wasn't the first time they had stood by our family in crisis, in prayer and loving concern.

Then in August of 1969, my son called me long distance with shocking news. A tornado had struck with sudden destruction; several friends were dead, others injured. Paul, the Brokke's thirteen-year-old son, was missing.

When I asked about Harold and Cathy, my son Marshall said, "I talked with Mr. Brokke today. Cathy, along with most of the others, was thrown into the lake. She's hurt, but she's going to be all right. Danny pulled his mother from the water. He's okay, too. The divers are still searching for Paul's body . . . But, Mom, I'll never forget what Mr. Brokke said to me, after he told me about it all."

"Yes?" I could hear Marshall's voice break.

"He said, 'Well, anyway—our God is a *good* God.' "

I was remembering how it seemed that all his teaching had focused on the Lordship of Jesus Christ, how often he had reminded us, when we had gone through deep valleys, that when the Lord puts His sheep out, He always goes before! Now he was repeating, from his own valley of sorrow, "God is a good God." The words had a greater impact than ever before.

Because they have no comprehension at all, the world often challenges Christians concerning the goodness of God. And when they do, I have but one answer.

"You say, 'I can't understand a God who is perfect goodness standing by while little children suffer and die, while disease, and poverty, and war take their toll of the innocent . . .'

"But I say, 'Knowing the kind of a person I am, how utterly unworthy, I can't understand a God who is perfect goodness who would love me enough to die for me.'

"I can't understand it . . . but that's what He did!"

"He hath hedged me about, that I cannot get out: he hath made my chain heavy." [1]

—*Jeremiah*

7.

Who Builds the Fences?

Maybe you've never felt a compulsion to run out of a situation you felt you couldn't cope with. But from what I've observed, most everyone at some time or other considers the only possible solution to their plight to be escape by running.

Escapism, in fact, has become a religion in itself in this day. Within the churches there are as many subjugated to this cult as there are on the outside. While those in the churches may resort to escape mechanisms less obvious and odious, they are predisposed to being AWOL from God's perfect will and purpose, geographically and otherwise.

So it was when I found myself in an impossible situation; I felt hopelessly trapped. There was no denying it; I felt baffled, too, because for all my prayers, I hadn't seen any evidence that the circumstances would get any better. There were two insurmountable fences which kept me from escaping—my physical condition and lack of money. Still I struggled. Surely there must be some way out!

Then one day the Spirit implanted this question in my mind: If the Lord is Lord and He is in control—who builds the fences?

Who builds the fences? Of course I knew, but I wasn't ready to admit it.

81

However, it wasn't long before one night in the after-midnight hours, the Lord took me through the Book of Exodus, reminding me how it had been with the children of Israel—and showing me how it was with me.

God had intended Moses' only credentials as leader would be, "I AM THAT I AM . . . I AM hath sent me unto you." [2] He wanted the people to accept Moses as their leader on the basis of one thing—faith. Had they been living in God, they would have needed no other sign.

Moses didn't know how important it was that they accept him on the basis of faith alone. And so in answer to his demand, he is given Aaron for a mouthpiece and supernatural manifestations which the people could see for proof.

Consequently, there was plenty of trouble ahead for Moses. And there were forty years of confusion for God's chosen people. Because they had been convinced by the signs, they lacked that quality of faith which could have taken them through the wilderness in only eight days.

When God first begins to work to deliver from the bondage of oppression, things often seem worse. So it was with Israel, captive in Egypt. Moses' first request of Pharaoh, for his people to go into the wilderness to worship, brought increased labor. Now they must search for stubble with which to make bricks. When they failed to meet their former quota, they were beaten. In anger they confronted Moses: "Deliverance! Moses, what sort of ballyhoo have you been promising us?"

Moses promptly took their complaints to God. Reassured by God of His everlasting covenant, Moses tried to bring assurance to his people, but they were so wrought up over their present distress, they didn't even hear him. They were looking within—rather than above. Since they weren't preoccupied with God, what concerned them was the trial of today—not the promise of the future.

They had witnessed God's power in the plagues which caused Pharaoh to finally drive them from the land. They had seen His power in deliverance at the crossing of the Red Sea. There had not been a moment when they were not traveling under God's visible protection—the cloud by day and the pillar of fire by night. There had been manna from heaven, and water gushing from the rock, but these people who knew miracle after miracle of God's provision soon forgot. Frustrated and angry, they cried out against Moses and Aaron: "Would to God we had died by the hand of the Lord in the land of Egypt . . . for ye have brought us forth into this wilderness, to kill this whole assembly with hunger." [3]

It was quite obvious they didn't see God as their leader. They had followed Moses and Aaron out of Egypt—not God!

Moses put it to them straight: "The Lord heareth your murmurings which ye murmur against him: and what are we? Your murmurings are not against us, but against the Lord." [4]

While I was reading the account of the Israelites, I was painfully aware of the Spirit making application to me.

In moving almost three thousand miles to the place where we were then living, we had not questioned God's leading. I was as convinced as my husband that God had appointed the time and place of our move.

But later, when we found "the straw taken away and we had to search for stubble to make bricks," I couldn't understand what was happening. The problems piled up and the tensions mounted, and I'd been asking, "Lord, what gives!"

By the time I got to the 16th chapter of Exodus that night, the Lord came directly to the point: "Just who did you follow out of Egypt anyway—God or Moses? Do you still believe I led you here, or did you come because of a man?"

I was trembling when I answered, "You—Lord . . ." I knew it had been so at the time.

"Then if you followed Me here—what are you complaining about? And why have you been struggling about the fences?"

Maybe you are thinking that in your situation it is not by your choice, nor have you ever had the assurance that this is God's place for you. Consider that Caleb and Joshua stayed with their people, being subject to God's judgments as well as His blessings. As they subjected themselves to the authority of God's chosen leader, they were under the authority of God, led every step by Him.

I had wondered how I could go on as things were. Months had passed, while the situation grew more difficult. At one point the doctor had stood by my bed in the hospital and said, "You can't go on like this. Whether you know it or not, you're right to the breaking point."

I knew, all too well.

Unless something changed, I couldn't go on under the stress of the situation. And so I began looking for a way *out*, rather than trusting the Lord for a way *through*. At first, it seemed wrong, yet at the same time, there seemed to be no alternative. Then I even began to wonder if I lacked faith to believe the Lord could take care of all that would involve my leaving!

It was such a subtle suggestion of the enemy. It frightens me now, to think back, because I realize that in toying with an idea which I knew to be contrary to God's will, I began to believe it was the right step to take. Things even began to happen to confirm the wrong as being right.

I remember a night a few months later when I was again in the hospital. It was nearly midnight, and one of the nurses, knowing I was awake, slipped in to talk to me. She knew nothing of the inner turmoil, the problems, or the decisions facing me. She mentioned seeing me reading my Bible, and began talking about the privilege we have of rolling all our burdens off on Jesus. She told me a little of the heartache she was, even then, going through; her child was dying of an incurable disease. She told how God was sustaining her, and then suddenly she paused and added, "He will give you grace to walk out of an impossible situation." I gasped. Was this the Lord's word to me? In the past few weeks, more than one door had opened quite unexpectedly to me. Was this confirmation? I was becoming more and more bewildered and also nearer to the breaking point.

I cannot tell you all the ways God used to change my thinking.

But I came to a crisis where I knew, if God did not do a miracle in my heart, I couldn't face another day.

In those early morning hours, as He put the question to me, "Just who is it you are following—Moses or Me?" I began to stop running.

He showed me the first thing I had to do was settle the question, once and for all, of who built the fences? Was I still going to keep trying to climb over them?

When I forced myself to admit that it was God who had, as Jeremiah put it, "hedged me about that I cannot get out," that whatever the situation—He had allowed it, I had also to face the fact that my struggle was not against people or situations, but against God. The physical limitations, the lack of money—these weren't the real issue; it was the Lordship of Jesus Christ. Without question, His Lordship had allowed the fences; His love had kept them high enough that I couldn't climb over. Until I really accepted this, I would never know peace.

I had to let go of resentment, thinking myself trapped, and start thanking the Lord that He had kept me secure, hedged in by His love. Whether or not I ever saw a change in those outside influences which had caused me such despair, running wasn't God's answer. I had prayed to be kept in the center of God's will. He built the fences to keep me from straying. There was no doubt about it.

Thank God, for the depth of that first crisis commitment to His Lordship—deeper than all the turmoil—and for the reality of that fact He made known time and time again. The moment I faced my own problem squarely, and confessed that in even considering escape, I'd been kicking the Lordship of Jesus Christ, I began to come out of confusion. Such was His mercy and love, continually teaching me His ways, and how to walk in them.

"Lord," I said, "sink or swim, live or die, I concede—You build the fences. And I'm settling it right now; whatever happens or however I feel, I'm not going to consider the possibility of a way out again. Though I'm interned in the valley of heartache by the fences, I'm staying where You put me. Here and now I'm reaffirming my commitment to Your absolute Lordship—right here in the valley. All that happens to me here is Your responsibility. The future is up to You."

It was a definite turning point! God gave me to know that He wouldn't let me break under the pressures. What the future held, I had no idea; but He gave me to understand I must never again look for a way of escape. I must look to the Lord alone who would bring me through every valley in victory. He was Lord in this valley too!

Whenever I'm prone to forget, I still hear Him ask, "Just who are you following—Moses or Me?"

Man forged the iron chains which had so often bound Paul's feet, and he was guarded by Roman soldiers. But there was no sense in which he felt trapped when the door clanged shut, confining him to his prison cell. Paul never considered himself anything but "a prisoner of the Lord." [5]

However, it wasn't when they locked the chains in place that Paul became a prisoner of Jesus Christ. It had happened many years before.

God had spotlighted Paul on the road to Damascus, and the beam which struck him down had left him blind. It was Paul's first experience in the valley—that one which brings us our first personal encounter with Jesus. Here is where the revelation comes that it is our own personal sin that drove the spikes into the hands and feet of the Savior. It was *my* sin that plunged the sword into His side; the spilling of His blood was an atonement for *me*. Paul saw his part. Confronted by Jesus, he discovered that in persecuting the church, he had actually been persecuting Jesus. One can never hurt those who are Christ's own without hurting Him more.

The totality with which Paul, lying there on his face in the dust of the Damascus road, believed and accepted Jesus, is attested to by the question he asks: "Lord, what wilt thou have me to do?" [6]

Paul was not merely concerned with the next twenty-four hours. He knew by what he had seen in those he persecuted, when he surrendered his life to the rule of Christ, his future would be marked for radical change. Paul wanted to know exactly what was to be the purpose of his life from that moment on—precisely what the Lord would have him do.

For three days of darkness, shut in alone with the Lord, during which time he neither ate nor drank, Paul saw the Lord's preview of what he could expect in the future. During that time, Paul was made fully aware of the "cost." [7] He spent three days in the valley. God didn't spare him the details of what he would suffer as a chosen vessel of the Lord—total identification, predetermined persecution.

How well he knew! If only he could forget the thud of stones, the bloody broken body of that young man they called Stephen, whose face had been as an angel, when just as he was dying he had looked up into heaven and said, "Lord, lay not this sin to their charge." [8] No! He could never forget!

Three days in the valley . . . It was there Paul accepted the chains. That was when he became a prisoner of the Lord Jesus Christ. From that moment on, his total submission to the Lord put him in a position where earthly limitations would always be inconsequential. For the rest of his life, faith, love, and obedience were the chains which bound him body, soul, and spirit to the Lord. Whether he was preaching to the Jews, standing before the king, ministering to the churches, on land or in a storm at sea, with Silas in prison singing a duet at midnight, or writing his prison epistles under the watchful eye of a Roman guard, he could say with all sincerity, "I, Paul, a prisoner of Jesus Christ . . ." Love and submission to his Lord held him far more securely than any imprisonment by men.

Throughout the whole Bible, we see it is common for God's most useful servants to spend time shut up in prison.

Consider the experiences of Joseph, Daniel, and Jeremiah, as they are related in the Old Testament.

Charged with a sin he didn't commit, by a woman scorned, Joseph was thrown into prison. "But the Lord was with Joseph, and showed him mercy, and gave him favour in the sight of the keeper of the prison. . . . The Lord was with him, and that which he did, the Lord made it to prosper." [9]

Later Joseph was able to look back and say to his brothers, "Be not grieved, nor angry with yourselves, that ye sold me hither; for God did send me before you to preserve life. . . . So now it was not you that sent me hither, but God." [10]

Daniel didn't worry over the king's decree which would cause him to be cast into the lions' den. He didn't open the windows; he didn't close them. He didn't send out an SOS to his friends to pray that the Lord would set fire to the decree or strike by lightning those who had been responsible for it. Neither was his communion with God interrupted. He simply knelt "three times a day, and prayed, and gave thanks before his God, as he did aforetime." [11]

Daniel's faith which shut the lions' mouths was born the day he purposed in his heart that nothing would deter him from serving the Lord God.

Jeremiah went through some terrible times of spiritual conflict. When Pashur heard that Jeremiah had prophesied the desolation of the Jews, he smote him and put him in stocks. The next day, he took him out, and Jeremiah continued to prophesy. In his frustration he cried out, "Because the word of the Lord was made a reproach unto me, and a derision, daily. Then I said, I will not make mention of him, nor speak any more in his name. But his word was in mine heart as a burning fire shut up in my bones, and I was weary with forbearing, and I could not stay." [12]

Jeremiah reached some frightfully low valleys when his prophesying landed him in prison again and again. He had been cast into the dungeon before, then removed to the court of the prison; but when King Zedekiah turned him over to the people, they put him into a dungeon where he sank down into the mire, and there was nothing to eat. Again he was rescued, this time by an Ethiopian eunuch who threw down old rags for him to use as padding under the armpits of his emaciated body, that the cords would not cut him as they pulled him from the bottom of the pit.

Jeremiah isn't describing any mountaintop, glory-all-the-way experience; his cries come out of the anguish he had endured in the valleys when he says, "He hath hedged me about that I cannot get out: he hath made my chain heavy." [13] Though in his despair he had cursed the day of his birth, later he looked back and saw that the Lord allowed all that had happened to him.

Whenever we find ourselves limited in the scope of our activity, surrounded by a seemingly impossible situation, knowing who is in control of our lives makes the difference as to whether or not we feel trapped, or whether we can accept—even when it seems without rhyme or reason—our captivity. What a difference it makes!

No, I don't always feel like thanking the Lord for the fences. There are still days when having been shut in much of the time, I feel closed in upon. But then I hear Him ask, "Who builds the fences?" and I turn to the Word and read again the verse He gave me as a promise at a time of great need. "It is God that girdeth me with strength, and maketh my way perfect." [14]

Only as I come to the Lord in complete honesty about my feelings, does He work to change them. Sometimes, I just have to say, "Lord, I know this is Your Word to me. I see nothing but the fences, but You have promised Your supply of strength and to make my way perfect. Whatever is changed, You'll have to change. I can't understand. I can't even change my feelings, but I can trust and with David say, 'My heart is fixed!' [15] And no matter what, I will not look for an escape route out of this or any other valley, for I know Your hand has led me here."

Life has brought other valleys from which I could hope to escape. But I have been learning that it is my attitude which makes me a prisoner of circumstances. God's love, which builds those fences, confines me as a prisoner-by-choice of the Lord Jesus Christ.

Trapped by physical limitations, by finances, by circumstances over which I have no control? No, not really, because I know who builds the fences, and I have His Word: "He that trusteth in the Lord, mercy shall compass him about." [16]

And my trust is in the Lord who builds every fence out of His mercy and His love.

"For me, to live is Christ—His life in me; and to die is gain—[the gain of the glory of eternity]. . . . I can say nothing as to my personal preference—I cannot choose, but I am hard pressed between the two." [1]

—*Paul*

8.

I Cannot Choose

I used to wonder how Paul could seem to imply a choice as to whether he stayed in this present world or departed to be with the Lord. I quit wondering a long time ago; I'm sure there have been many times I could easily have stepped over that line at will.

Over forty times in the hospital, some times no one thought I would walk out; the violent hemorrhages, finally forcing me to submit to three lung operations in ten months; other complications; the wearing struggle to keep going in spite of the pain, to care for my family—this had been a dominant part of the pattern of my life.

I had walked the borderline so often that my acceptance of God's will—whether it was life or death—wasn't some hypothetical possibility to regard with apathy or shove into the future. I knew what the score was, and I had settled that issue a long time ago, had summed up the disposition of my desire in a thousand-and-some prayers: "Whether I live or die—let Jesus Christ be glorified!"

My children were committed to the Lord before they were born, and they've never been taken off the altar. But that doesn't mean there have never been any struggles when I faced the possibility of leaving them motherless—nor paradoxically, periods of frightful depression when I felt they would be better off without me.

However, life doesn't remain static. Each year the physical demands of caring for the three boys became less; they were more and more help; and I was making fewer trips to the hospital. Then there was the coming of their tiny baby sister, the darling of all our hearts. Nevertheless, certain problems were replaced by others, and sometimes I wondered why the terrain of life was sliced with such deep valleys.

Exposure to the revelation of Jesus as Lord had left no question that His rule was absolute. My rights? If He was Lord, I had none. It was a divine confrontation, but then I had no concept of what must transpire before that knowledge became my own personal experience. Even so, to come to the place where I was willing to let Him assert His claim to certain areas of my life had been a terrible struggle. Never had I known such conflict. I thought I had already walked through the valley of submission, but this valley experience was three months long, without parallel to anything I had ever passed through before. At long last, I looked up to the One whose side had been pierced, who bore the nail prints in His hands and feet, and I meant it for time and eternity when I whispered, "My Lord, and *my* God."

From then on life has been lived on a different plane. Even though it was no grand finale, from then on everything which I touched or which touched my life, was related to that committal. There are ever new claims of His Lordship to be met; the valleys don't become shallower, but deeper and darker, as we move on from faith to faith. And always victory means complete identification with Christ in spite of the circumstances. But there can be no daily victories unless there are daily battles.[2]

And so it was I looked back over one of the most difficult years I had yet known. There had been the strain of financial pressure, personal heartache, emotional stress, and I had been very ill. That spring the doctors had told me I wasn't fighting to live anymore.

They were right. I was so utterly weary; I wanted so desperately to go Home. The only thing which held me to life was my little daughter, five years old at the time. Yet in God's dealings with me, I had settled it: if He did take me Home, I could be sure He had something better for my little girl.

I had been home from the hospital three days. Beside me on the bed, my *Amplified New Testament* lay opened at Philippians, chapter one. The 20th verse had long been underlined in blue, later marked in red. Beside it, dated when I had written them, were these words: "Only the work of the Holy Spirit has made this prayer real to me: 'Lord, spare me not—only let Jesus Christ be glorified!!!' "

". . . whether through life or death . . ."

Just before I'd left the hospital, one of my doctors had taken my hand and said, "I don't know what the situation is, but I've sensed something—not something I can say, 'I know,' but I want you to listen to me. This is my philosophy: A saint is a saint in *any* situation, and a sinner is a sinner in *any* situation."

While I had never shared with him any of the pressure and the problems facing me back home, there was no doubt; God was using my Catholic doctor to remind me that what we are in God is unaffected by people or situations—a saint is a saint in any situation. Of course, he was right! But I didn't feel very saintly right then.

And now that I was back home and the situation remained unchanged, I felt even less like a saint.

When a minister friend came in to see me, I shared with him some of God's dealings during the past days and weeks.

"It wasn't easy to commit Jan to His keeping if it meant leaving her motherless; yet I've always known she belonged to God, not to me." I handed him my open Testament. "The Lord has been bringing me back again and again to that 20th verse," I said, then added wistfully, "Maybe He's getting ready to take me Home."

The minister leaned back on his chair and folded his arms.

"Maybe He's just getting you ready to live."

I closed my eyes, the tears spilling over in a rush. *Getting me ready to live? But Lord, I'm so tired, so weary. How can I go on?*

Now he was reading the passage I had pointed out. I listened while the tears continued unabated. *That verse.* But he didn't stop. "I can say nothing as to my personal preference—I cannot choose . . ." [3]

Just then I felt the smile of Jesus, the warmth of His smile enveloping me! He said, with such tenderness, "You know it's not enough to say, 'Yes, Lord . . . I cannot choose!' You have to smile back—even through the tears."

I began to feel myself relax.

After turning some pages, the minister went on reading. "Thank [God] in everything . . . for this is the will of God for you [who are] in Christ Jesus." [4]

In everything? The pain, the tears, the loneliness, the heartache, the endless struggle for breath? Not afterward—but in the midst of everything give thanks! And smile back, "for this is the will of God in Christ Jesus" for me.

My mind suddenly began rerunning the "what if's?" My little girl? No, I couldn't keep back the tears which streamed, but I could say, "Yes, Lord, she is Yours. And I want my love for You to become a consuming fire that will burn away every other love—every cherished dream—everything—until there is only an eternal flame of love for Jesus." There aren't any *"what if's?"* if He is really Lord.

Who can will these things in themselves? Who can be sufficient in himself?

Not me—that was for certain! But I could still feel the warmth of His smile as I whispered, "Yes, Lord—I can and do choose to put my will on the side of God's will, even against myself when they clash—even the natural desire of a mother to raise her daughter, if it is not to be. Let me live from day to day with only the strength You give, one breath at a time, taking 'the cup' from Your hand and giving thanks.

"No, Lord, I can't of myself—but I can trust Your choice for me as being best, and smile back and say, 'Yes, Lord!' Even when others see only the tears, and they never know, You see the smile on the inside."

No, "I cannot choose!" But "in everything" I *can* give thanks!

Each day the Lord was drawing me closer to His will. Next He spoke through these words of Paul: "We were so utterly and unbearably weighed down and crushed that we despaired even of life [itself]. Indeed, we felt within ourselves that we had received the [very] sentence of death; but that was to keep us from trusting and depending on ourselves instead of on God Who raises the dead. . . . He will still rescue and save us . . . and draw us to Himself. While you also co-operate by your prayers for us. . . . Thus the lips of many persons Godward turned will [eventually] give thanks on our behalf . . ." [5]

In that which God had called me to do, I had despaired, for in the natural it was absolutely impossible. But the Lord was making it plain that He had let me hit rock bottom, like Paul, until I "despaired of life itself," for the same reason—to keep me from trusting and depending on myself instead of on God.

There was the assurance that if I utterly depended upon the God who could even raise the dead, He would rule and overrule to accomplish His purpose. And because others had prayed, they would share in the blessing of seeing Jesus Christ alone glorified.

A couple of days later, my own pastor spent the afternoon with me. Harold Irish knew the struggle I was going through. As we were talking about the Scriptures through which the Lord had been speaking to me, he began reading again from Philippians. Suddenly he looked up and exclaimed, "But you didn't read far enough. Listen to verses 24 and 25: 'But to remain in my body is more needful and essential for your sake. Since I am convinced of this, I know I shall remain and stay by you all, to promote your progress and joy in believing.' "

He stopped and put it to me straight. "Can you keep on saying, 'Yes, Lord'?"

What else could I say? I knew the Lord was putting the words in

his mouth. He wasn't just picking a promise for me at random
which I could latch onto.

He went on. "Can't you see? He's asking you to be willing to remain and minister His love. Because of the overwhelming problems, you've considered that verse 23 would be such a blessed escape. We've talked before how from day to day you are going to
have to learn to live in Christ's body. Now He is saying: 'Are you
willing to live in My body, to keep trusting moment by moment no
matter how deep the hurts, and keep on showing them My love?'"

Someone had said to me, "We get the altar built to the Lord,
and then turn around and it falls down."

I knew I had been building an altar, stone by stone as the Lord
handed them to me—each stone a commitment to the Lordship of
Jesus Christ in a specific thing. I began examining the stones of the
altar I had been building. No! I knew better. The altar doesn't *fall*
down if it's erected unto the Lord at His direction. I am the only
one who can topple the altar that I have erected to the Lord. And
God forbid that I should pry one stone loose!

I had been saying, "For this reason I'm holding onto life." The
Lord was saying, "Stop saying, 'For this reason only . . .' There are
others to whom I want you to minister My love. Can you accept
them, and desire just as much to hold onto life until you fulfill My
reason for your accepting My will?"

Not until much later did I come to realize that I was trying to escape the cost of total commitment by giving up the will to live. But
this I did understand. God had clearly indicated that I had no right
to any preference—life *or* death. It was not up to me to choose.

If I could not choose, then there was only one way. Whatever
ministry God ever gave to me, now or in the future, would be in
utter dependency upon Him. And love must flow to all men without preference, because it would be His love. Anything which was
not resurrected by Him would be of death and not of life. Moment
by moment—breath by breath—it is imperative that I draw from
His resurrection life.

In so doing, I have the promise of Jesus that no matter how my days are spent, if they are lived in Christ, they shall be marked by the only absolute, infallible, exclusive evidence of the Holy Spirit: "He shall glorify Me." [6]

And so God has transferred that prayer written in the margin of my Bible into reality through experience.

"Whether through life or death . . ." I cannot choose! Yet He does continue to fulfill the supreme desire of my heart as He leads me through the valleys.

My prayer: "Lord, spare me not—only let Jesus Christ be glorified!"

> "I laid me down and slept; I awaked; for the Lord sustained me." [1]
>
> —*David*

9.

He Maketh Me to Rest—in the Valley

It was one of those days when I didn't have the strength to keep going any longer. It bothered me most that it was Saturday, and there was extra work to be done. My sixteen-year-old son would do a good job, I knew, but I didn't enjoy lying in bed hearing the washer running, the pans rattling in the kitchen, the little noises that reminded me he was left alone with it all to do since he was the only one of the boys home that day. I was almost too sick to care. Yet I was fretting on the inside because I couldn't be up working with him. It was impossible though. I didn't have the strength to do anything but lie still. Slowly I rolled toward the window. I must have slept.

When I had been in the hospital a couple of weeks before, my pastor had given me a devotional booklet by Haddon Robinson, based on the Twenty-third Psalm, the cover lithographed in beautiful natural color. At the time the Catskills had blazed with the same bright hues; as far as one looked in any direction, aspen, maple, and birch flamed red and yellow. But they were beginning to fade, the leaves wearied by the winds which swept down the valley. Through the window, I could see what had been one of the most showy maples of all. Now it looked as listless and bedraggled as I felt.

Awake now, I reached to draw the booklet from others piled on the bed beside me. There were few pages I had not marked, underlining those thoughts which had been particularly meaningful.

Surely the best known of all the psalms, none is more beautiful than this song of David. My mother had taught me the Twenty-third Psalm long before I started school.

Memorizing Scripture is one thing. But try living it! Some find it easy, others find it hard to commit words to memory; but regardless of how that may be with you, if you wholly commit yourself to God's words, you'll find following through on that commitment won't always be easy. He will lead you right down through some valley experiences which you never dreamed existed.

Take just the first five words of the Psalm. Underline the little word *my*. Trust yourself to the Spirit's technique to transpose those five words from the printed page—to imprint them indelibly in your heart—that you may never again take the Lord's name in vain by claiming false identity.

If you're like me, you won't make it beyond there without wondering, at least once in a while, if you shouldn't have been content to enjoy the words in the Book and not have prayed so fervently that they would become your meat and drink. You'll also learn experientially something of what David was talking about when he declared, "What time I am afraid, I will trust in thee." [2] And no matter how frightening the experience, if you do trust Him as Lord in the valley, you won't know defeat. You'll walk out in victory!

The Shepherd's Psalm . . . I opened the little book at random. I was more rested now, but still restless inside. I wanted to be up and doing. The first words I noticed were those of David himself. "He maketh me to lie down in green pastures . . ."

Although I could say, "The Lord is *my* Shepherd . . ." and knew I was committed to His Lordship, I had a lot of learning to do. And I was learning now, right now, while I was lying under the ruling hand of the Lord. And I didn't like it!

"Just who is making you to lie down?" It was the Shepherd's voice, gentle but firm.

The words stared back at me. "The Lord . . . He maketh me . . ."

I grew quiet, very quiet inside.

"Yes, Lord," I whispered. "You are."

His Lordship!

There was no other answer.

Several years had passed since there had been that climactic experience when I had embraced Jesus Christ as Lord. One of the first of His claims to me then had been that of Shepherd. Submission to the Shepherd meant I must be willing to be led, even bled.

There it was: "He maketh me to lie down . . ." I had said it so many times: "If He is really Lord, the only answer I can ever give is 'Yes, Lord!' and smile back. Everything is from his hand!" *Oh? Even this?*

"But Lord, where are the green pastures?"

When I ask such insipient questions, I'm often conscious of His patient smile, as I was when He answered, "White sheets, no less."

I couldn't help smiling back at that.

"Okay, Lord. I understand. It is You who 'maketh me to lie down.'" A wise, loving Shepherd forcing me to needed rest—the green pastures were between white sheets.

How many times I've made my little ones lie down because I knew they needed rest, even when they didn't think so.

"Now would you listen and let Me do the talking? Just be still and listen—that's why you're here—I want to talk to you today." One thing I have learned: when the Lord stops me short like that, I'd better pay close attention. Class is in session!

"He maketh me to lie down . . ."

Rest and listen! The sounds from the other part of the house drifted through the closed door in muted tones. The necessary work was being done, and I thanked the Lord for a son who was so capable; that he was there to care for his little sister who adored him. Yes, over all, the Lord was in control, even if I wanted to be and wasn't.

Throughout the entire day I drifted in and out of sleep, but always there was that pervading consciousness of the presence of the Shepherd. Even now I can sense the wonder. How can I explain it? The transcendent, wordless communication of His love, the reassurance that He was perfectly able to control every area of my life, and this was His gracious desire. Willing submission and confident trust were all He asked of me, and neither involved activity.

"He maketh me to lie down in green pastures . . ." I was so weary. I desperately needed rest. And the Shepherd knew.

"Rest and listen . . ." It was Jesus!

There have been many, many similar days when there have been so many things I wanted to do, so many plans, and things which I thought demanded my attention. Yet they were all beyond my strength. Sometimes, all I could do was lie with my head on the pillow. Nothing more. But even so, I have found that rather than being times of restless frustration, such times can be rewarding times of spiritual renewal.

It would seem that there are some ministrations of the Spirit peculiarly realized only when the soul is at complete repose. Perhaps, for some, sleep affords the only time when the human spirit becomes quiet enough to receive from God. "Those who have the gale of the Holy Spirit go forward even in sleep," wrote Brother Lawrence. Said the Psalmist, "He gives (blessings) to His beloved in sleep."

We need times when we can separate ourselves from the noise and flurry of living, when nothing demands our immediate attention, when we are only "tuned in" to hear God speak. If there is no other way, the Shepherd may lead us down into the valley where we are forced to accept the quiet resting place. But I have found that when He makes us to lie down, He is very near. For God neither leads nor restricts by remote control! Isaiah declares, "He shall feed his flock like a shepherd: he shall gather the lambs with his arm, and carry them in his bosom, and shall gently lead those that are with young."

A word of warning though. It is one thing to be set aside from doing things, and another to escape behind the shut door. In either case, however, the remedy is in listening to the Shepherd's voice, and then in doing what one is told.

The learning which comes from such an experience is priceless, the Spirit of God taking familiar words out of the Book and making them come alive. The Shepherd had issued the orders—rest and listen—because he knew exactly what the sheep needed. And because He was *my* Shepherd. He was there!

But He had something more for me that day. Unless you have known long periods of illness, you may not understand the shifts of mood to which the sick are subject. As night came on, I was suddenly overcome with the feeling that no one, not even those closest, really understood how it was. Such a feeling of desolation is apt to swamp us shortly after we have heard God speak. I am sure that it comes from having a heart filled with what God has given, and the desire to share cannot be realized because there is no one who would understand.

Still there was the warmth of His presence. Again I heard the Shepherd's voice: "I understand! Isn't that enough?"

I picked up my notebook, and words came almost as fast as I could write. Throughout the morning I had been rankled that I couldn't be up and doing. But when I let go, how precious had been the ministry of Jesus. And He was ministering still.

At the end of an unforgettable day spent alone with the Shepherd, He was giving me words to express all I had been unable to express while exhausted by pain and lack of sleep. I wrote in the glow of His presence, the Spirit confirming that His sufficiency did meet every need of the submissive heart.

I didn't have to answer when He said: "I understand. Isn't that enough?"

I had His answer! I share it here:

Is It Enough?

Is it enough to know—He knows
When nights seem endless, long, so very long
the wearing pain
the restlessness.
No human hand to hold
Nothing to which to lash my faith
But Him—and that He knows,
Is it enough?

Is it enough to know—He understands
The deep, deep longing of my heart to do and give
of strength
and means,
to those who've given so much to me.
Instead, I'm forced to add my burden to their load
And He says: "Give MY LOVE!"
Is it enough?

Is it enough to know—He knows
When life seems but an endless maze
to those who watch
and sneer:
"Where is your God Who loves?"
And I alone, can hear the Voice
that says: "I led you here."
Is it enough?

Is it enough to know—He understands
When I've no strength to even cling
to Him
His nail-pierced hand.
But e'en must let Him stoop to pick me up
And sobbing out my heart to Him
just lie there helpless in His arms.
Is it enough?

Is it enough to know—He knows
The future, how and when the end will come
for me.
Yes, Death.
To know He's been before–and it was then
He wrung the hinges from hell's gates
to give to me eternal life.
Is it enough?

Is it enough—enough, you ask
to trust to Jesus Christ, to One I've never seen
this life of mine
completely His.
Enough? There are not words enough
to tell just what I feel, how much I know
For I have felt His smile. I'm His, you see—
It is enough!

"I sat not in the assembly of those who make merry, nor did I rejoice; I sat alone because Your . . . hand was upon me, for You have filled Me with indignation." [1]
—*Jeremiah*

10.

Alone with God—in the Valley

I sat staring out the window at the Catalina mountains which ring the north of Tucson, feeling every bit as spiritually barren as their smoky brown rock-jutted slopes looked in the blue desert haze of late afternoon.

"Why? Why, Lord? Why do I always seem to have to face the hardest places alone?"

Before me on the table was an old notebook. Idly I flipped its pages, while my thoughts were taken up with pickings from the past. So often it has been like that, I thought. It wasn't that I was out of touch with people; there were friends and family. But some feelings are too deep to communicate, an inner aloneness which no one person can dispel.

Then I came across these lines I had written long before I knew much about the vitriolic pressures of life. I read:

> *Lord, I do not seek an easy path*
> *To journey on life's way—*
> *A way that leads through fields of green*
> *And through the cool of day;*

Where flowers bloom, and birds sing
 And breezes softly blow
Where merrily my friends may walk
 Mid sunlight's glow . . . with me.

But Lord, I pray that Thou wilt lead
 Up rough and narrow pathways steep,
O'er mountain trails, and hillsides bare
 Through dark ravines, and valleys deep
Where gales and storms may sweep my soul
 And in the night and all alone,
Save for Thy guiding hand on mine
 I brave the dark unknown . . . with Thee.

I had been asking "Why?" But I'm afraid I smiled rather grimly when He answered, "I took you at your word."

God had been answering my prayer, in different ways, and over a lifetime. He had taken me at my word.

Had I asked God for something more than I was ready to receive? Sometimes when the storms and gales had swept my soul in the midnight blackness of those valleys, all I had been able to cry was, "O God!" But always, in that moment of anguish, I knew everything I needed was communicated to Him.

I've often thought back to the services we attended in the old Riverside mission hall; the hard wooden-slatted benches, the soiled, limp, manila-backed songbooks, the faces . . . And although I couldn't have been more than six at the time, I can even now remember what it was like as we sang:

The storms of life around me beating,
 And rough the path that I may trod
Within my closet door, retreating,
 I love to be alone with God.
Alone with God, the world forsaking

Alone with God, Oh, blest retreat
Alone with God, and in Him hidden
To hold with Him communion sweet.

Child though I was, I wasn't just joining in singing this beautiful old hymn. This desire toward God was a part of my very being reaching out, longing for personal communion with my Creator. Whether it was at this time God planted the seed of this intense desire, I do not know. But whenever it was, God continued to nourish it. The prayer which became a part of me was, "Lord Jesus, take me into the depths alone with You!" I know this prayer was born of God!

Certainly, as a child, I had no idea for what I was asking in praying thus. Before you ever even consider praying such a prayer, you should know that it will mean the deepest valleys. It will mean God taking all your crutches. You won't only leave others behind, you'll come to the end of yourself.

The farther Jesus takes us into the depths alone with Him, the darker it becomes—the more His glory is revealed. There is nothing that can compare with the presence of Jesus in the valley, either in times of heartbreak or in knowing His glory.

God knew in praying thus I was not asking Him for just an experience. I wanted this to be the whole tenor of my life. And so He has answered—dramatically at times—and I have often struggled violently against the answers. But He is ever there to remind me: "This is what you asked for. I took you at your word." In the midst of the struggle I've often told the Lord to ignore the tears. But never have I told Him to ignore the prayer. As long as He gives me breath, even when the flesh rebels, I want nothing less than to go into the depths with Jesus.

Since then, the deeper revelation of the Lordship of Jesus Christ, and the ensuing response of my heart touched by the Holy Spirit, makes me determined that He should rule every area of my life. In progressing from faith to faith, I find the revelation expanded. I've been made aware of the reciprocal action that is the sequence of

God's call—depending upon acceptance or rejection of divine light and love. In all, I have been shatteringly exposed to the sovereignty of God, and that He has ordained us to have a part in His eternal purposes.

You don't travel this way long before discovering that the farther you go with Jesus, the thinner the crowd gets. For if you desire a depth of communion beyond the ordinary, Jesus will take you into a place, shut in alone with Him, where nobody else can go . . . just Jesus and you. He will, for the reason that Love responds to love.

Often Jesus left the multitude behind to be alone with just the Twelve. There were many things He wanted to say to them that He couldn't say to the masses. Time was moving swiftly, and there was so much to teach them. Again and again, He had taken Peter, James, and John and spent the hours alone with these who had shown the greatest comprehension of the nature of His Kingdom. In anyone who will come apart alone with Him and open his heart, He will implant His deepest truths. Jesus said, "It is your Father's good pleasure to give you the kingdom." [2] He will, if we are willing to take the time to separate ourselves unto Him.

Though the demands upon Him were incessant, Jesus frequently slipped away alone to be ministered to by His Father, to draw strength for what lay ahead as well as for daily need. If He needed to do so, how much more do we. Who knows what lies ahead for which we must be prepared? But whatever the enemy's onslaughts against us as we draw nearer to the end time, the time to discover our resource in God is now!

As the pressure built up that last night before His betrayal, Jesus sought the fellowship of prayer with the three dearest to His heart. They had crossed the brook Cedron and entered the garden where they had often prayed together. But they didn't pray together that night. "He went on a little farther," [3] and they went to sleep.

However, in the despair and darkness of those hours, He was not alone. He had known how it would be, for He said, "Ye shall be scattered, every man to his own, and shall leave me alone: and yet I am not alone, because the Father is with me." [4]

Communion of Father and Son was sharing the painful knowing of the indescribable agony which each would endure in the hours just ahead. In those hours of anguish, encompassed in His Father's love, Jesus was able to see the whole spectrum of Calvary. Though sweating great drops of blood, He was able to say, "Not as I will, but as thou wilt." [5]

We can't begin to comprehend what total abandonment by the Father was like, as Calvary became the revelation of God's wrath. But because He knew, it is the extreme of loneliness which we therefore need never suffer.

Once we embrace His Lordship to the limit, however, there will be a driving compulsion to be alone with Him. Jesus will give us the privilege of going on a little farther with Him. There will be our own personal Gethsemane. And Calvary.

But there will be no place where He hasn't been before. No matter what—He knows!

What transpires in the heart in this valley, makes the difference between the mere mouthing of words and the true spirit of submission born out of love for God, whenever we say, "Not as I will, but as Thou wilt."

We aren't to go around looking for situations and circumstances out of which we can build ourselves a cross. People do try. But we are told to take up the cross Jesus gives us to bear, not to build one of our own design.

The aloneness God calls us to is by no means a life of cloistered withdrawal from human contact. Although it is a realm of the Spirit, it is by no means some mystical ideology.

There is simply no one to lean upon, only Jesus. But in this valley alone with Him, I look up and cry, "Nothing in my hand I bring, simply to Thy Cross I cling!" [6] "I dare not trust the sweetest frame, but wholly lean on Jesus' name!" [7] It has happened, while I was being brushed against by the crowd, or thrust aside by the "brethren."

Sometimes I have had to bear a deep, deep hurt, knowing that it could not be shared. When God seals these things in our heart, in this too, Jesus forces us to meet this call and commitment to Him alone—if we want this very special relationship with Him.

Even after praying so long in this direction, I came to a time when God ploughed such a deep furrow in my spirit, that He exposed that this lifelong desire was also something I had greatly feared. It didn't seem possible! Yet there was no hedging the fact that it was so.

At the time, I was in a place where there was almost no spiritual fellowship with other believers. I knew loneliness, aching loneliness. In seeking the Lord, as He had been dealing with other problems in my life, I had an inner consciousness that I was not getting down to bedrock; there was still something short-circuiting the flow of God's love in and through me.

As to what it was, I honestly didn't know. Then while I was waiting before the Lord, the faces of a couple came before me. I had leaned heavily upon these two through some desperate hours. However, I knew that if I gave the Lord full opportunity to work in my life, it could well affect our friendship. Some of what He might do, would certainly be contrary to the doctrines tenaciously held by these two. It was not that I would not be able to accept them if they did not understand what God was doing. But I doubted they would ever accept some things of the Spirit. It had taken the Spirit a long time to bring me step by step to this place. I treasured their friendship. Without it there would be practically no one with whom I could have spiritual fellowship. Could I stand a broken relationship here?

Deep within, I knew there could be only one answer. Jesus was calling me to complete aloneness with Him—His Lordship. His heart of love would never be satisfied with anything less, "because he delighted in me." [8] And "I am my beloved's and my beloved is mine." [9] No one can share the sacredness of that love!

The Lord didn't ask me to give up these friends. He did ask me to be willing to let Him do whatever He desired, not holding back

for fear it would cause misunderstanding between us. He reminded
me of still others who would be estranged from me. I knew how
deep-rooted the prejudices; there were bound to be other hurts,
and certainly voiced censure, if in totally yielding to Him, I was
brought into certain new dimensions of His grace.

But I also knew that when the test comes, my love for Jesus and
total commitment to His Lordship would always hold supremacy
over every other love—family, friends, relations. If it meant being
rejected by any or all, my loyalty to Christ still came first. It included my letting Jesus lead me in ways which might well leave me
without a single one who understood.

The words became a rhythmic beat: "The servant is not greater
than his Lord." [10]

The disciples had not understood, that night in the garden, when
Jesus went beyond them a little to be alone with His Father. Three
times He came back to find them sleeping. Alone, He wrestled
through the night, in agony of soul. Alone, He faced the horror of
Calvary. But He had set His face to do the Father's will, and that
took Him far beyond all human fellowship.

I know much the Lord has allowed in my life has been to teach
me utter dependence upon Him. The lessons have not been easy.
But His love has been necessarily ruthless to hold me to my commitment and to establish that relationship where I learned to appropriate His strength and His supply for all my needs. Such a commitment covers a lifetime of choices, choices which shut me up to
God alone.

In all of this, I'm well aware of the danger of thinking oneself
into a "separate class." The aloneness Jesus calls us to does not
draw one apart from the fellowship of believers nor the reaching
out to unbelievers; rather it opens the channel of love to all.

If there is to be separation, it will be of God, because we have
moved in the flow of God and He has channeled the stream.

Commitment to going on a little farther, is a commitment of un-
quavering trust in the Lordship of Jesus Christ over every situation

—regardless of people or circumstances. It means recognizing His voice when surrounded by the crowd and no one else hears or is aware of His presence.

It means keeping the counsels of my heart.

Especially, to me, it means going directly to Him, trusting His promise that what we ask in His name He will do. It means not allowing anything to be hidden—all exposed to Him.

It means sharing the Triune love of Father, Son, and Holy Spirit —an intimate relationship, dependent not upon geographical location, being with other believers, in the midst of the multitude, with a chosen few, with just one other person, or with no one at all. It is that inner indwelling of His Spirit which nothing on the outside can touch.

Alone with the Father, Jesus made that final testimony of commitment to His Father's will, "Not my will but thine be done." The carrying out of that commitment accomplished all that would ever be necessary to reconcile me to God—that I might be "accepted in the beloved," [11] and know this intimate relationship, alone with Him.

In that hour, the darkest the world has ever known, when the veil of Christ's flesh was rent by a sword, God rent the veil of the temple from top to bottom. Now all men might enter the holy of holies of God's-temple-within to be shut in with Him alone. Until then, only the high priest could have this relationship once a year.

So it is that Jesus, Himself the blood-sprinkled mercy seat, bids me move in to be at home with God. While such an act defies human comprehension, yet through faith, I understand I am no longer on the outside!

It is that glorious fact which gives me the impetus, the grace to be willing by faith, to walk in the Spirit beyond the crowd and the little groups of close friends and family, to where the last human tie is broken and they are all behind.

Whatever or whomever He takes from me leaves me defenseless and dependent.

But I've learned to appreciate God's allowing me to come to this place, for in His intimate presence, there can be no hurt. He alone is perfection. Here there are no broken idols, no confidences broken, no promises broken, no broken trust. And there is the conscious flow of the Spirit, His overflowing supply.

Alone? Forsaken?

When you are conscious only of His presence, He can reveal Himself beyond the ordinary. He will begin to discover you to yourself. And if you discover your place in Him, you will be able to smile back even in the dark, in the loneliest valley, and say, "Yes, Lord. You are all I need. My life is hid IN CHRIST. And I am complete in Thee." [12]

"I am going to boast only about how weak I am and how great God is to use such weakness for his glory." [1]
—*Paul*

11.

Weakness Becomes an Asset

Who hasn't had his own particular world suddenly explode in his face and been mightily shaken by the repercussion? Haven't you stewed over the best way to deal with troublesome factors which have kept the pot boiling, riffled through problems, even while knowing you weren't going to come up with any surefire solution, found yourself caught in a situation somewhat like being caught on third base in a squeeze play, or been knocked down and out for the count; your work piles up, but you haven't the strength to rebound and get with it?

This is the way it was with me when I was hospitalized a good distance from home. Everything added up to make me decide I possessed as much spiritual fortitude and was as useful to God and others as an ice cube sitting on the north pole.

After talking out some of what was involved with my pastor on the phone from the hospital, I tearfully blurted out, "And here I am— So desperately weary of it all, yet too weak to do anything about it!"

I could hear a soft chuckle. "Now wait a minute, Florence. Suppose, physically, you were strong and in good health. Tell me—just what more could you possibly do about the whole works?"

114

I was forced to smile. The answer was glaringly obvious. Absolutely nothing! Prayer would still be my only recourse.

"Well?" I could hear the lilt to his voice, but I knew he was pressing me for an answer.

"Roll it off on the Lord . . ."

We laughed, the tension broken. He knew the Lord had been crowding me into a corner where I was forced to utter dependence upon Him, that the situation demanded it, and that I had to reject any notion that I could "help" the Lord out in any way—even if I had been strong.

My pastor well understood God's workings in the valleys. Having more than an ordinary understanding of what the Lord was doing, he cared enough to always put it to me straight and to remind me that my commitment to the Lordship of Jesus was a commitment to a way of life, a life of submission whatever the circumstances, a life under His rule in which problems, situations, family, and myself were all His responsibility.

Throughout many difficult months, the ministry of Harold Irish was to me, a special favor. Harold knew I didn't want a "tactful" pastor: I wanted an honest one. When it came to spiritual problems, we didn't just make talk; we settled issues. I could always level with him and knew he would level with me, no punches pulled. And he did just that on the phone that night.

But long-term sickness and physical weakness can deplete the inner resources of resilience. When there is no creative outlet for the mind, and inside you're chafing at the bit to be pulling your share of the load, it's easy to accumulate a lot of erroneous suppositions—such as being able to handle situations, keep your own little world wound up and running smoothly, and being able to fight spiritual battles with more going for you—if only you were in good health.

If you long to be serving in some specific capacity as a Christian, and are unable because of restricting causes, whether illness, binding responsibilities, lack of ability or training, or whatever, you may well feel like excess baggage.

If you fail to meet the claims of the Lord here, you're headed for disaster. As always there must be an unqualified submission of personality, temperament, natural abilities, or acquired skills, strength or weakness, to the Lord; if He uses any, all, or none, that's His business.

Especially, with a severe physical problem, if you begin to think of yourself as being good-for-nothing, you're apt to start stacking up the problems on the inside. You're plagued with the urge to be up and doing. A million and one things, more or less, demand your immediate attention, or so you think. And yet you can't adequately accomplish even one. So what you can't do on the "outside," is transposed into restlessness, stress, and worry on the inside. It's like a logjam above a bridge, and just as treacherous.

How often I've heard the Lord say, "Carry the load if you insist. But when you put it down, it will be unchanged; you'll be more weary, though." And He was always right.

I knew well my propensity for carrying burdens, while He stood by waiting for me to roll them off on Him. I knew that I was forever trying to "help" the Lord. Physical weakness wasn't easy to accept when life held so many exciting challenges. There were so many needful, legitimate things to be done, in addition to the necessary work in caring for a home and family. Of course, there was the other side of the picture also—days when I didn't have enough energy to care if I ever accomplished anything.

Finally, I began to realize the Lord hadn't taken me down into this valley just so I would learn to accept the limitations of my physical condition and other restrictive circumstances. Definitely, the Lord had something more in mind. So I began asking to know what this valley was all about: what exactly was the Lord trying to get through to me?

Lounging in the recliner one day with all the vim and vigor of a rag doll, I heard His voice. "Don't you know? Your weakness is an asset—not a liability!"

I thought that one through backward and forward and turned the words inside out: weakness an asset, not a liability?

Then the Lord added the restrictive clause, "*If* you turn your weakness over to Me. My Lordship makes all the difference."

I'd been challenged to faith and been lifted up by Isaiah 40:28–31 over the years. I'd certainly known the Lord's provision in the 29th verse: "To them that have no might he increaseth strength." But to consider weakness as an asset seemed stretching the point.

Paul often zeroed in on his weakness being the receptacle into which the Lord poured His strength; always, that in whatever he did, the glory would be Christ's alone. But that was Paul. And what he said was, no doubt, out of modesty and humility. I just couldn't conjure up a picture of anything weak about Paul!

But in the Lord's dealings, you learn to go to Him and to the Word until you have His answer and your heart is at peace.

So I did, and discovered that in his letters to the Corinthian church, Paul had stressed no less than nine times that in himself he was weak. His authority, which they questioned in establishing the church at Corinth and his subsequent ministry, he declares, was the unqualified supply of God's wisdom and strength supplanting his own foolishness and weakness. He was nothing: God was everything.

Experience had taught Paul that the less he had to offer in the natural, the more the Lord was able to supply. For the more he saw himself as utterly weak and useless apart from the Spirit, the less he injected himself in his preaching or in his actions, and the more the Lord injected His strength and wisdom. There had to be a need before the Lord could fill it. And the need was met to the greatest extent when Paul felt the weakest. When he ministered in the strength of the Lord, then was his "weakness perfected." Through total submission to the Lord, Paul was used by God to accomplish His maximum purposes.

I had to give in! Actually, it didn't make an iota of difference whether Paul had a build like Hercules or Pinocchio. His spiritual ruggedness wasn't related to physical strength, nor could it be touched by physical weakness. Come to any conclusion you might as to his physique, infirmities, or "thorn in the flesh"; in themselves, they weren't important. But whatever stripped Paul of all confidence in his own ability or strength, forcing him to rely upon the inflow of God's power, was all important. Therefore, weakness did become an asset as it brought him to know the superabundance of God's strength enabling him to meet situation after situation in the power of God and for the glory of Jesus Christ.

Here I had been thinking, *I've no reserves left—nothing.* Even walking the short distance into the bedroom to rest seemed too great an effort. And now this had come from the Lord.

I couldn't help chuckling.

"Okay, Lord. If weakness is an asset—not a liability—I don't know what I've been complaining about. I've got it made!"

The Lord had gotten through.

To Paul, He had said, "My strength is made perfect in weakness." [2] And Paul's inspired self-analysis causes us to know Paul learned in time of need the interchange of God's strength for his weakness. To me, the Lord had said, "Your weakness is an asset, not a liability, if you turn your weakness over to Me." Just as He promised, I've found that whenever I do, His strength does supersede my weaknesses.

The summation of what God was teaching me is beautifully expressed in the song which has sung itself in my heart in many such valleys.

When we have exhausted our store of endurance,
When our strength has failed ere the day is half-done;
When we reach the end of our hoarded resources,
Our Father's full giving is only begun.

When Satan assails and temptations grow stronger
And often we feel it is too much to bear;
In weakness we learn of His infinite Power—
His grace is sufficient; our Father doth care.

His love hath no limit, His grace hath no measure,
His power hath no boundary known unto men;

For out of His infinite riches in Jesus
He giveth and giveth and giveth again.[3]

Even when my world had turned upside down and I was flat on my back, this still was to be my confidence: "That in everything ye are enriched by Him, in all utterance, and in all knowledge . . . so that ye come behind in no gift; waiting for the coming of our Lord Jesus Christ." [4]

Whatever was accomplished for the Lord, it wouldn't be because of my being stronger, smarter, more clever, or persistent than the next fellow. To consider victory in spiritual battles being at all contingent on physical strength was absurd. Weak or strong, sick or well, we know that whatever the odds stacked against us as seen by the grandstand, the answer is always the same if He is Lord: "The battle is the Lord's." [5] Faith is the victory that overcomes. "For the weapons of our warfare are not physical (weapons of flesh and blood), but they are mighty before God for the overthrow and destruction of strongholds. [Inasmuch as we] refute arguments and theories and reasonings and every proud and lofty thing that sets itself up against the (true) knowledge of God; and we lead every thought and purpose away captive into the obedience of Christ, the Messiah, the Anointed One." [6]

When our thoughts are brought under the rule of Christ, it follows that we do roll the burden off on Him, for our responses reflect who controls our thoughts.

No matter how difficult things seem, whenever I am ready to honestly admit, "I can't do anything on my own. I need You, Lord. Do what you want, only let Jesus Christ be glorified!" thereby turning my weaknesses, physical and all the rest, over to Him, I can be assured that my weakness becomes an asset.

If I didn't need God's strength, I would never know His supply. If the Lord didn't allow those situations which demand His wisdom and working to bring about a solution, I'd go on staggering around under the load. You know why? Because I don't want others to see how really weak I am. I want to appear as a bulwark of faith, when

I am really nothing. But nothing about me is changed by what any-one thinks, either good or bad. I am only what God sees and knows me to be.

Since I have come to this understanding, and have turned my weakness over to Him, I've released the Lord to pour His strength into my being, body, soul, and spirit, to accomplish what would be absolutely impossible otherwise. And I am learning that depen-dence upon the Lord for strength which sets me free from what *I* am.

For no matter who or what we are, at the top or the bottom of the ladder, with energy to spare or too weak to raise our head off the pillow, we need the wisdom and work of the same Holy Spirit. When we no longer consider the quality of our being, but reflect our confidence in His Being, "such trust have we through Christ to God-ward: Not that we are sufficient of ourselves to think any thing as of ourselves; but our sufficiency is of God." [7]

Thus I find continual release from my strengthless self into the inexhaustible energy of the Omnipotent, not necessarily energy to be expended in activity, but the energy of faith that enables me to move with God.

"May you be able to feel and understand, as all God's children should, how long, how wide, how deep, and how high his love really is; and to experience this love for yourselves, though it is so great that you will never see the end of it or fully know or understand it. And so at last you will be filled up with God Himself." [1]

—Paul

12.

Being Understood or Understanding Him

Mother tells that when I was a very little girl, we had a visitor who, I sensed, didn't like me. After she had left, I was unusually quiet and thoughtful. Even as a child I loved most people, and it bothered me when they didn't respond by loving me. My dejection plainly showed when I finally admitted my hurt feelings to my mother.

"I don't think she liked me very well," I confided. Then I suddenly brightened. "But I think if she knew me better—she'd like me better."

Such is the naïveté of a child!

Now that I'm older and wiser, I'm quite aware that if she had known me better, she might have liked me less.

Somehow, we feel if only people knew the real us—the person on the inside—they would accept us even as we accept ourselves, with all our faults . . . since we understand, at least in part, the whys and wherefores of how we act. Besides, most of us have a stock of seemingly reasonable excuses for any unseemly behavior, which we're sure, if we could explain them to others, would make us acceptable.

No one likes to be misunderstood—unless we're overrated. Then our flattered ego may accept the overrating as the recognition of our true worth.

Having our good intentions misjudged, though, especially by someone we particularly care about impressing, hurts. And if, perchance, we're caught in a tanglement of circumstances and feel we're being blamed unjustly, we find ourselves repeating, repeating, repeating, "But you don't understand!"

I discovered the hard way that the more I tried to explain things from where I stood, the more confused the situation became. I hadn't known the Bible warned, "If I justify myself, mine own mouth shall condemn me: if I say, I am perfect, it shall also prove me perverse." [2] My efforts at self-justification had always failed to restore harmony or bring understanding. It simply was not God's way!

There is nothing wrong with wanting to be understood. Jesus recognized the need of the human spirit for understanding. And those who follow Him are to communicate compassion, minister comfort, show forbearance, reach out in love and understanding, whatever the problem. Within the Body of Christ, all needs should be met through mutual fellowship and communion. And yet, often they are not. Wherever you go with Jesus—within the church or out, into broken homes, to the brokenhearted, to the desolate and the lonely—"understanding," you will find to be an acute need common to all humanity, a need which is seldom satisfied!

It has been pointed out that most of the people who end up in mental institutions would not be there if one single person had been able to communicate love to them, to make them believe someone cared and understood the pressures and problems with which they had been unable to cope.

The church can meet the need of those suffering mental and emotional problems only through you and me as individuals filled with God's love. They need to know His love channeled through a person. But if you cling to one trace of the pharisaical manner which has mistakenly been equated with spirituality, you'll never reach through to them. Fling out the trite, "Get a hold of yourself," or "Pull yourself together," and doctors warn, it may be the final straw. Neither will you impart hope by a pseudo-spiritual, "Jesus is the answer to all your problems."

Despair has become, to the mentally ill, an obsession, because they already feel there is nothing to which they can hold; everything is out of control, no one understands how it is. To be lashed with advice, and then left to find *how* He's the answer, only causes deeper and deeper withdrawal. And no matter how well meant, the advice crowds them closer to the brink of a complete breakdown.

For me, it has always seemed when I've needed the understanding of friends and family the most, there has been no one. This I've had to accept. Who can understand the physical pain of another, the sleepless nights which seem forever, the pressure from the problems sickness creates, the emotional upheaval within over family problems, even the desire to escape that can overwhelm one at times?

But these are the very things God has used to teach me utter dependence upon Him. To transpose head theology into heart experience, I have been taken into valley after valley where I have been stripped of all the props I normally could count on. Only here did I learn to appropriate the all-sufficiency of God. Even to know His understanding was enough.

Once when I so desperately wanted someone with whom I could share my pent-up feelings, I kept thinking, *If there was only one person to understand* . . .

Then the Lord put the question to me: "Just what do you really want them to understand? That right now you are feeling awfully sorry for yourself, and just how much you are guilty of self-pity?"

"Oh, no Lord. Not that!"

"What about the resentment when you are unable to do the things you want to do, because of your physical condition? How about the times you have used your illness to escape responsibility?

How about bitterness? Or that there are other deep-rooted resentments? Or that you aren't as spiritual as you try to give the impression of being sometimes. Just how much do you really want others to understand? All of this?"

Of course not! I wanted them to understand what a rough time I was having—the fears and frustrations. But I also wanted them to understand that I was a much nicer person than what they saw on the outside. I was looking for human understanding to bolster my morale, and to be quite frank, I was looking for self-veneration, too.

The Lord still wasn't through.

"If you were really honest and allowed the Holy Spirit to reveal the truth, you'd make a solemn discovery—not a very flattering one, either. What you really want is not for others to understand what you really are nor the depth of your feelings, but you want them to picture you like what you wish you were!"

I cringed under the impact.

Joseph's brothers made a desperate appeal to him that he understand their plight when they went down into Egypt seeking food. Not recognizing who he was, they carefully guarded their guilt when they spoke of the brother who "was not." They wanted him to understand their father's loss of a son, that he would take pity on him and on them, but they didn't want him to know that they were responsible for the old man's heartbreak. They never dreamed that Joseph well knew who and what they really were.

Even so, we desire understanding that will cause sympathy but not censure, disregarding the fact that God sees the hidden motive: He knows us stripped of all our sham.

We cling tenaciously to the desire for someone to understand what we are going through (which may come out of a martyr complex), why we behave as we do (so they will know that we are a product of our background and excuse us accordingly), and our motives (we meant well, and we don't want to be falsely accused). We want them to be aware of our hardships, all we've been forced to endure. (Again: Jesus never said it would be easy!) And we certainly want others to know how we feel about certain issues; they need to be set straight. If only we could explain ourselves, whatever the problem, to just one person who would really understand, they would appreciate our position and we would find consolation. Or so we think.

We forget Jesus said that misunderstanding and false accusations were to be expected, but that "Blessed are ye, when men shall revile you, and persecute you, and shall say all manner of evil against you falsely, for my sake." [3]

At other times, we try to put into words that which moves us deeply, yet we know we aren't getting through, we aren't being understood. In this too we can become frustrated. And we will be, until we realize it isn't our job to convince or convict. But even when it comes to the legitimate desire and need for human understanding, God wants this need supplied through human relationships only up to a point. Therefore, He puts us in situation after situation where we have no one with whom to share, where there is no human consolation, where we are forced to accept His understanding as enough.

The Lord showed me that since there would always be an innate desire for human understanding as part of normal personality, He would take me again and again through this valley. For He wanted me to know when He was seeking to shut me up to Himself alone. Not that He would not have those along the way who would minister in compassion and love and in that understanding which they would receive from the Spirit of God, but I was not to look to them for understanding. That would be quite futile, for genuine empathy in the natural is a rare virtue possessed by few.

The more we are shut up to God alone, the more we will become sensitive to the needs of others, for God's desire is that we in whom Christ dwells should be an oasis to those in the wilderness of despair.

When God told Ezekiel he was to carry a message of warning to the children of Israel who were in captivity, Ezekiel gritted his teeth in rebellion. Later he admitted, "I went in bitterness, in the heat of my spirit; but the hand of the Lord was strong upon me." [4]

It was distressing enough that the Spirit should so whisk him away and set him down by the river among the captives, but then to be forced to sit in absolute silence among them for seven days— God wanted Ezekiel to be able to identify with their plight before saying one word. No matter what message we minister from the Lord, He doesn't want it contaminated by "the heat of our spirit." Ezekiel needed seven days to get calmed down before God would even let him open his mouth that he might speak of God's coming judgments.

One can't truly feel for anyone while sitting on the sidelines looking on. This God knew. Ezekiel says of his forced "sit-a-thon," "I sat where they sat." [5] Seven days! Only then did God give him the message for these people.

Paul told the Christians at Corinth that the only possible way they could minister in compassion was to enter into a new realm of knowledge through the love of Christ indwelling them. This knowledge would not even be related to ordinary human understanding. There is a marked difference when "the love of Christ constraineth us . . . wherefore henceforth know we no man after the flesh." [6] Once we begin to see each other as spiritual creatures, we'll be quicker to accept the responsibility of Paul's admonition to comfort those who are fearful and to comfort and forgive those suffering remorse for their sins.

We read: "Blessed be God . . . who comforteth us in all our tribulation, that we may be able to comfort them which are in any trouble, by the comfort wherewith we ourselves are comforted of God." [7]

Stripped of all human understanding, I learn to rest in God. "He knoweth the secrets of the heart; [8] the prayer of the upright is his delight; [9] the Lord knoweth them that are his." [10] Assurance of His perfect understanding, and receiving comfort from Him, He tells me, are for sharing with others in their time of trouble.

However, there came a day when the Lord said, "You have longed for understanding, but it is far more important to realize that my heart yearns for you to understand Me!

"This is what I really want, that you understand My motives, My mercy, My purposes, My joy, My peace, My grace, My holiness, My righteousness, My position, My manifold wisdom, My heart of Love, My Promise in the Person of the Holy Spirit, My provision, My desires—and the understanding must come through the dealings of God in valleys far deeper than any you have known before."

It is frightening and yet exciting to know that God is working in us. He doesn't want you or me to be the hub of the wheel where we are the center and we are always relating everything—people and events—to how they affect us. Rather, we are to be a spoke which reaches out from the center, or even the rim which gets scrunched in the gravel, as the Kingdom of God moves on with Christ at the center.

In His Kingdom, everything relates to Jesus. We must understand this. We will never know anything but confusion, turmoil, a completely disoriented life, and a woefully distorted view—looking from the center out. But if Jesus, the conquering Christ, is at the center—looking from the outside in to Him makes all the difference in physical, mental, and spiritual well-being, and in our spiritual perception.

Jesus spoke of the Holy Spirit as the Comforter. It was important that His disciples should know His presence would always be with them to comfort and direct. There was no limit to His understanding of their most mundane needs. But the main thrust of His ministry to His disciples was to reveal Himself and establish His Kingdom within their hearts. His purpose in calling them to follow Him was that they might know Him.

To me, Jesus never made a statement more charged with pathos than those words spoken to Philip which seem to be wrung from

His very heart: "Have I been so long time with you, and yet hast thou not known me, Philip?" [11]

Jesus had something more in mind than acquaintanceship. He was looking deep within the man.

That the masses who followed would never see beyond the miracles He performed, or if they accepted Him, they would accept Him as no more than a good, kind teacher or at most a prophet, He expected. But He had exposed His disciples to the most poignant impulses which motivated His every word and act. He had shared all the Father had given Him to ready them for the time when He would leave them, that they might go on to complete His purpose in their calling. He had sought to teach and discipline those who were His own, to the point where their spirits would be synchronized with His Spirit. He had fervently prayed that they might have a divine depth of understanding, which had quite obviously not yet come to fruition in Philip.

For over three years He had not spared Himself; in every way He had tried to get through to the Twelve, *who* He was. To have Philip give evidence of so little comprehension of all He had taught them concerning His Kingdom must have been as a stab wound, piercing deep.

How much had any of them grasped?

"Oh, Lord," I prayed, "I don't know what it may mean, but don't let me be 'so long time with You' and then have You say, 'Yet, hast thou not known Me?' I long to know You, to understand Your desires, Your purposes."

Surely the Lord wants to be our refuge in the "hurts." But in His Lordship, we find so much more than a refuge. He wants our communication with Him to be more than that between a loving Father and a troubled child.

I so often think of Mary Magdalene. In Mary we have a graphic example of the Lord's willingness and power to transform one possessed by seven devils, into the Mary who followed Him about the countryside, ministering to Him and providing for Him out of her own personal possessions.[12]

Again and again we find another Mary at the feet of Jesus, learning, worshiping, serving, breaking the box of alabaster and anointing His head and feet, wiping them with her hair. She alone knew what the Master really wanted.

The disciples stood around grumbling that she had "wasted" the precious ointment that could have been sold and the money distributed among the poor. But Jesus knew what pure love had flowed from the one who sat at His feet. Tenderly He said, "She hath done what she could." [13]

The disciples were operating out of the natural reasoning of the mind, the intellect, at the level of the soul. Mary operated out of the spirit, the pure expression of her love. She had seen beyond to where Love called to love, and she had responded accordingly. Only when there is in us the same quality of love as that which possessed Mary, will the Lord allow us to see beyond the veil of natural reasoning!

Jesus said, "Wheresoever this gospel shall be preached throughout the whole world, this also that she hath done shall be spoken of for a memorial of her." [14]

Even so, with Mary Magdalene. From what she was, to what she became—it happened as she stayed close to Jesus and kept her heart open to what He really wanted. No wonder Jesus appeared first to her after His resurrection. Mary could not bear to be parted from Him, even after what seemed the finality of personal relationship, when her Lord was sealed in the tomb. She had asked only the privilege of sitting at his feet and being near even in His death.

It was no coincidence, I'm certain, when I found myself in the hospital sharing the room with a dear little Catholic lady, eighty years old, who had come to the United States from Lithuania in 1904. Her name was Mary Magdalene.

A short while before, she had suffered a stroke which made it necessary to have her long hair cut to shoulder length. She told me that until then, she had never had it cut in her entire life, not even bangs as a child.

She said, "I hoped Jesus would someday give me the privilege of washing His feet with my tears and wiping them with my long hair." I could have wept at the beauty of such faith.

I said, "Mary, I don't know *how*. But don't worry. If you have always loved Jesus that much, someday He will give you that privilege! If you love Him that much, I know He will!"

Those days we spent together were rich ones for me. Often we repeated the Lord's Prayer or the Twenty-third Psalm together. Sometimes we simply blessed the Lord together. As I would stroke her hair, so very soft, back from her forehead, she would repeat over and over, "Blessed be the name of Jesus!" Believe me, the presence of Jesus was there!

Sometimes she would become frightened in the night, and I would slip out of bed and over to her, holding her hand, reassuring her that she didn't have to be afraid, because Jesus told us when we trust Him we have nothing to fear. I reminded her that He was holding her hand—the Shepherd was always in the valley with the sheep. And always she would quiet down and say, "Oh, yes. Blessed be the name of Jesus!"

One day she said, "Wouldn't it be wonderful if we could all go Home to Jesus together?"

I said, "Yes, but Mary, if you get to see Him first, you tell Him I'm coming." I wish you could have seen her smile.

I saw little spiritual life in the rest of her family. She had gone far beyond them in her love for Jesus. I prayed that the Lord would take her quickly to Himself, since I saw what the future would hold for her in her paralyzed condition. And she had such tremendous expectancy of faith.

I wanted so much to be with her when she went Home. But it wasn't to be. And it was very hard leaving her when I was discharged from the hospital. When I went back not too long after, I asked about Mary Magdalene. The nurses told me that she had simply gone to sleep soon after I had left. My heart was flooded with praise, for I knew that when she awoke she would be at His feet, looking up into the face of her Lord, her lifelong hope at last realized.

Mary taught me so much about worship, real worship, the special communion which can be ours when we come to understand what it is that Jesus desires, when our Life is wholly directed toward fulfilling that desire. Often when I reached out to her in the night and heard her whispering, "Blessed be the name of Jesus," I would hear another Voice deep within: "This is why I'm taking you through these valleys. That you might learn to know Me, to understand My heart's desires."

Yes, there have been times since when I have wept because the valley was so dark and there was no human hand to hold, no one with whom to share, no person who understood. But always, as I quit trying to substitute the hand of a person for the all enfolding love of God, I know the presence of the indwelling Christ. Never is a valley so dark He is not there.

Understanding no longer seems so important, not since knowing Mary Magdalene. Born of that experience has been my prayer, "Lord, don't let my motivation in knowing You ever be the same again. Let me be more thrilled with my quest for You and in seeking the building of Your Kingdom within, than in anything else ever!

"Keep my heart aflame with the same desire that burned in the breast of Mary Magdalene and the other Mary, nearly two thousand years ago, and which shone so gloriously bright in the dear little woman who also bore that name. Thank you for bringing Mary into my life that I might learn more fully to say, 'Yes, Lord,' to every valley that brings a deeper understanding of You and Your desires.

"Let me always rest in knowing that You do understand, but let me be motivated by the one consuming desire to understand You, that I may satisfy the heart of God."

"The captive exile hasteneth that he may be loosed, and
that he should not die in the pit, nor that his bread
should fail. But I am the Lord thy God . . . And I have
put my words in thy mouth." [1]

—*Isaiah*

13.

Getting Rid of the Hang-ups

That we can desire God so desperately and still dig in our heels
when He starts moving us Godward seems incredible. But dig in we
do. That we should react to many of God's dealings in this way, I'm
sure stems from deep-rooted fears of which we may not even be
aware.

When there are these hang-ups, we have to get determinedly
honest with God and with ourselves before God can work to rid us
of all that would preclude His renewing a right spirit within. Until
we do, we will continue to be without freedom to receive from
God, to worship, to minister.

Knowing how often there has been this opposing action within
me to the deep workings of God, for long I have prayed, "Lord,
don't pay any attention to the tears and the skid marks, just please,
don't ever stop working till you conform me to the image of Jesus."
And so He has worked in spite of me.

If our desire is nourished through prayer and the Word, and we
genuinely do want to be transformed, God will bring those circumstances to bear which will accomplish His purpose. He has marvelous ways of fulfilling a sincere desire to know Him. One real mark

of spiritual progress is when the pressure of circumstances causes us to relax and say, "This is God!" and then to be sensitive to what God seeks to do.

For years I struggled against the baptism in the Holy Spirit. A lifetime of prejudices came out of what I had been taught and what I had seen manifested in the lives of those who claimed this experience. I had witnessed scores of heated arguments as both "contenders" and "defenders-of-the-faith" flayed each other with their own personal concept of what happened on the day of Pentecost and whether or not it was relative to today. The participants usually came out mangled, the grandstand was hardly edified, and I, for one, would carry the scars on the inside for a long time to come.

As time passed, I thought I had settled the issue for myself by refusing to identify with either camp. I could smile condescendingly at either side and say, "Of course, the Bible teaches it. I believe that the baptism in the Holy Spirit was the secret of the power of the early church. *Tongues?* Sure, if it's genuine." Under my breath, I generally added through clenched teeth, "But I don't need it. I have Jesus, and I'd rather not have anything connected with tongues than be around what I've seen demonstrated by those who claimed to have 'the baptism' along with this gift."

But God challenged my warped attitude. He confronted me with speaking in tongues which I could not deny was genuine. He let me live in daily contact with those in whom the Spirit had so manifested Himself; I knew their lives were marked by the consistent presence of God. However, this was only an interlude followed by experiences far more bitter than any I had previously known, leaving me even more baffled and cynical. Still, God was persistently working in me to build a sound structure. Therefore He exposed me to the extreme limits of those conflicts my mind struggled to resolve, proving I had never really settled the issue. I'd just been putting on a front while determinedly whistling in the dark.

But the time came when God called my bluff!

The only way it could ever be really settled, would be for me to submit to the Lordship of Jesus Christ as the Baptizer in the Holy Spirit. God knew my acceptance must be based solely on sound scriptural premises and personal application by the Holy Spirit. Everything else I'd known was debatable. Therefore what He'd been determinedly doing through these assorted past experiences, was wresting away every tendency to judge the baptism in the Holy Spirit by people or their actions. He caused me to become so confounded, I was left with the only infallible evidence to take account of: the Word of God.

Only that which is deeply rooted in the Scriptures ever becomes a permanent work of the Spirit, unshakable in crisis. I'd known this to be true when it came to other claims of His Lordship. The only concourse for me to the reality of any personal experience would have to be God's anointed Word.

It took me a long, long time to admit, even to myself, that it wasn't the Baptism, *per se,* I was struggling over, it was *tongues.* My manner of praying was just as absurd as if someone said to John the Baptist, "I want you to baptize me in the river Jordan for the remission of my sins, but please, don't get me wet." I was telling Jesus I wanted a "dry" baptism—No tongues, please!

Still, I couldn't eliminate it from my thinking. In trying to rate its importance, if any, to the church today, or whether it was pertinent to my own spiritual life, I was continually plagued by the question, *"What good is it?"* And as long as I based that question on my own observation, it was a well-founded, honest question. Then when I least expected it, I was abruptly faced with the biblical answers to my question, and for any true seeker, what God reveals to us in His Word belays argument. I knew I could never again with an ounce of honesty ask, "What good is it?"

It wasn't easy to slam the door tight on past prejudices and refuse to peek apprehensively through memory's windows while I searched out other facets of this truth in Scripture. Of course, I already knew the history of the early church. Brought to birth on the day of Pentecost, it had a phenomenal growth and outreach, which I had been taught could be chiefly attributed to the persecution it suffered.

Persecution from the outside had been a powerful dispersing agent, but I discovered a far greater internal stimulus.

The vital-motivating-force-of-Jesus which forged the New Testament church in unquenchable flame and which nurtured and established early believers was the baptism in the Holy Spirit—with its supernatural and scriptural manifestations!

Herein was the fulfillment of the promise Jesus made just before His ascension—that at the appointed time He would receive from His Father THE PROMISE (the Holy Spirit) and pour the Spirit forth upon those who waited in faith to receive. The immediate evidence was a tremendous new capacity to worship God: they were given an unlearned language, the Holy Spirit expressing through their human spirit the ultimate in worship and praise. And thus immersed in THE PROMISE—clothed over with the Holy Spirit—these worshipers would become witnesses with power to the whole world!

The church—believers unified through the Holy Spirit—was always to be a power-packed witness to the world. And Jesus gave every evidence that the gift of the Holy Spirit was for the church of every succeeding generation. But I would have preferred persecution alone to be the divine dynamo! It seemed being a martyr for Jesus Christ for more conventional reasons was more in accordance with my line of thinking and certainly more generally acceptable.

A minister friend, learning of the long years I had struggled with the whys and wherefores, the fears, doubts, and prejudices, asked me pointedly what I felt the chief hang-up to be. I blurted out, "What I have seen in Pentecostal circles!"

He drilled right in. "What specifically did you see?"

Well, I had seen plenty! But as memory turned over certain incidents I could have related, each seemed like a wisp of vapor when placed parallel to verses I knew by heart from the Word of God. It suddenly seemed ridiculous, stupid, and petty even to mention them. Sure there were memories that cut deep—I'd seen churches and homes split right down the middle, love and respect turn into bitter hate and contempt. My own heart had been trampled, my spirit ground in the dust. (Chalk up some of what happened to personality quirks, attempts to gratify the flesh, lack of proper teaching, lack of wisdom, lack of anointed authoritative leadership, misunderstanding of the Word of God, and certainly lack of love.) No, I couldn't forget what I'd seen, nor the hurts, but as I considered relating what I had seen, I was stripped of an answer. I felt frozen inside. I had nothing to say, nothing to relate! I didn't understand why.

A little while later, when I was alone, I cried out, "Lord, I honestly didn't know what to answer. What are You trying to say? What is really causing the hang-ups? I have to know!"

Get really desperate with the Lord. Get honest! I promise you He won't leave you in the dark long. But be prepared—you are quite likely to start squinting in the light, more than likely to be devastated when He flips on the switch. However, it is not only the first step, it is imperative in getting rid of the hang-ups in any area of your life, to face clearly the underlying causes in the light—to see as God sees these things!

'It happened to me the moment I cried, "Lord, I have to know!" God flipped the light switch to *On!*

My first impulse was to grab my pen. Often this is the way He communicates with me. I picked up a sheet of notepaper on the desk before me and began to write.

A new revelation? Hardly! Years before it had been painfully uncovered by the Spirit, but now it became related to what I had been using as an excuse. A cancer that prevented spiritual health and growth was that disposition which cried out for attention and enjoyed illegitimate recognition. This terrible tendency had been instilled through circumstances and background, and nourished by my harboring it through the years. Again, God was scraping up the mud; I saw its clinging tentacles revealed, how it affected my attitudes and actions. How often I had known, in the limited ministry the Lord had given, whether in a small way or in the miraculous, that which had begun in the Spirit had ended up in the flesh.

But then God showed me that implanted in the very depth of my being by Him, a Divine gift, was a holy fear and awesome respect for the sacredness of the things of the Spirit. I knew they were not to be tampered with lightly! I had a horror of playing with the unquenchable fire of the Spirit!

Now I understood the real hang-up! It was not any particular incident, not a person acting on impulse in the flesh, not the noise and exhibitionism I had revolted against which was the basic problem. But over and over I had witnessed the frightfully tragic outcome when those who had experienced the Holy Spirit's glorious manifestations failed to keep their hearts purged from all that would mar or corrupt this holy gift, when there was no holy reverence of these things.

This was what I had seen that really frightened me! Why? Because I realized what was in my own heart! Consequently, I was afraid to receive for fear that the unholy thing within me would contaminate and pervert that which was holy—and the end for me would also be tragedy!

Paul warns that one of the basic premises of the wisdom of God is that "no flesh shall glory in his presence." [2] For one baptized in the precious Holy Spirit of God to do and dare in the flesh apart from the Spirit, or to touch in any way the glory, I knew to be both dangerous and a stench to God! So I was just plain scared to receive, knowing my own inner weaknesses and bondages. I was afraid I would bring grief to God's heart and damnation to my own!

I stared down at what I had written . . .

There was no question the answer before me was from God. I knew by its clarity. Was I still scared? Every bit as much! The fears were still real, the hang-up still there, but I knew that now I could go give an honest answer to that question.

Admitting the truth wasn't easy, but God used that confession to give more insight into that as well as other hang-ups blocking the

free flow of the Spirit in my life. Within, I felt my own spirit beginning to settle. It didn't matter that I was still traveling through the
valley on a road pocked by chuckholes, that I was painfully shaken,
that I couldn't see around the next curve—I was on my way, and I
wasn't looking for a parking place or a place to make a U-turn!

Actually, the Lord had been pressing me hard into this corner for
months. Through illness, through circumstances, He was working
to destroy the weapons I'd been using in self-defense for "personal
survival." I didn't want to lose my identity in God. I'd built up
quite an arsenal.

The process of purging continued through the ministry of the
Word, through God's servants, through the voice of His Spirit
often awakening me from sleep.

"This is the way it has been. Are you willing to confess this too,
laying it bare?"

There were days when I was too weak to do anything but "lie
down" and "be still," but Jesus never paused in His ministry to me.
There was no fine print to be skipped over lightly, nothing but
stark reality when He showed me the cost. I had struggled almost
to the point of death over two specific issues: I wanted a discount
on the price tags, but the only reply was, "Were my LOVE less, the
cost would be less!"

HIS LOVE! It was the only thing of which I was sure. In my rebellion, I was forfeiting the only true security I had ever known, the
security of God's love revealed to me in Jesus. Whatever the cost,
was not He the all-sufficient source of strength and supply?

The pity was, like Paul, I had thought there was virtue in holding
stubbornly to the concepts I had grown up with.

How marvelous God's mercy! Even in my weakness and confusion, the Lord continued to minister in compassion, reassuring me
through past promises, imparting a growing confidence born of
God. He would never allow anything to touch my life which did
not come to me screened through His love. I didn't have to be
afraid of anything. I would never take a single step He hadn't taken
before.

Over and over came that gentle assurance, "I'll never push you. You need walk only as fast as you can without stumbling." No matter what the valley experience, His love had brought me here, and nothing could ever separate me from the love of Jesus. The valley of God's dealings was the manifestation of God's mercy. When I saw this, my spirit could respond with Paul's, "Thanks be to God, which giveth us the victory through our Lord Jesus Christ." [3]

However, He showed me the qualifying factor was my willingness to open my whole being to Him without any reservations for purifying through faith and the anointing of the Spirit. The conditioning process He had been putting me through was all working to this end. Still struggling, I cried out in desperation, "Lord, conquer me for Your Kingdom—at any cost!"

The saturation point of spiritual frustration comes when we have both a revelation from God of our need, and His more-than-enough provision to supply that hunger and thirst, yet we have not been delivered from the hang-ups which keep us from receiving. Precisely the way it was with me.

But God was in no hurry.

There was so much unlearning to do, so many new things He was teaching me. I was too exhausted mentally, emotionally, and physically for the Lord to work in any other way. Yet the utter weariness made me desperate to receive complete release of spirit. And there was being created within a craving for a capacity to worship and praise which I didn't fully understand, but which I knew Jesus could and must give. He does not create hunger to leave it unsatisfied.

Sometimes in my impatience to understand, trying to reevaluate Scripture divorced from personal theory or doctrines of men, I would almost despair of ever knowing experientially what it really meant to worship God in spirit and truth. My thoughts ran a treadmill. Intermeshed with Scripture was the rationalizing of long-collected, diversified, and controversial advice as to how to appropriate this provision of His grace. The treadmill kept spinning, and I would feel the frustration and mental pressure building up to a frightening level. Yet I came to know that at this point of mental weariness, I would always hear Jesus whisper, "Rest, child!" It meant refusing to even ponder the spiritual! Just rest!

This wasn't the way I had been taught a person would receive anything from God; one must pray through, trust, believe, do something. Surely one must take some action—anything but rest.

But I was learning. Rest meant to cease struggling. It involved a whole new concept of communion with Jesus. God knew that even as my body needed sleep at regular intervals, so my spirit needed to learn cessation of all activity. I didn't have to figure anything out. I discovered God wasn't working against any deadline in the conditioning process. He was going to take me clear to rock bottom, clear to the bottom of myself, and He doesn't work in haste at that depth.

The necessary conditioning process would take time. I was not to become impatient with myself, nor let anyone shake my faith because what God was doing with me was different in method from their "experience." He was, in His love, accommodating Himself to my own individual need which He alone could see in full perspective.

Repeatedly He warned me that I must not for a single moment pick up the memories out of the past which had worked to produce the bondage of fear in the first place. Each day would be a new beginning, and I was to be concerned only with the lessons of that day. Resting and listening!

While I was stretched out on the bed one day, the Lord reminded me how He hadn't let me hedge the question, "What do you think is the chief hang-up?" He'd given me the answer straight. Since then He'd been continuously clearing out other fears and bondages. Now He was ready to deal with that hang-up which still overshadowed them all, the one I had been most afraid to face. Why the unreasonable fear? Because I'd made it so complicated. He made it so simple.

He asked, "Do you know beyond any doubt that you belong to me?"

"Yes, Lord."

"Then if I live within, are you not indwelt by My Spirit? Surely you have the assurance of the outworkings of the Spirit in your life."

"Yes, Lord."

"Then you have trusted My keeping power if you do not question the reality of your relationship to Me."

Then came the loaded question: "What of all the precious things I have already done in your life? Surely any divine work of grace is holy. Why have you not been afraid of these gifts and manifestations becoming perverted or corrupted by what you have seen and feared within? And yet you are afraid to be immersed in the Holy Spirit."

I understood . . . and wept!

Certainly I had known times when I knew I was speaking and acting in God through the indwelling Spirit. At other times, I knew it was my human spirit acting on its own, and the result had been chaos, confusion—mental and emotional—and physical distress. Yet I had been scared to receive of Jesus Himself, the very Source of power for walking in victory, for witnessing. I had been afraid to yield myself completely to Jesus, to receive the greatest Promise given to His own, the gift of His Holy Spirit, just as it was outpoured on the day of Pentecost.

It was a new dimension of spiritual life which He longed for me to enter into. It broke my heart to think how smug I had been in my religious rebellion against this gift of love. I needed this work of the Spirit to keep every precious thing God ever did or would do in my life—in saving me, in filling me, in whatever way He would ever use me, whether shut in alone with Him or in witnessing—from being marred or perverted by the flesh.

And so God mercifully dropped a curtain on all that had gone before; it no longer had any bearing on the present. I wanted only God, without any limitations. Everything within me cried out that God would intensify that thirst which would drive me to Jesus who alone could satisfy my deepest and most desperate needs. I longed to respond to Jesus, who speaking of the Holy Spirit, cried, "If any man thirst, let him come unto me, and drink," [4] even as one dying of thirst in the desert would respond to a glass of clear sweet water pressed to his parched lips. Only the Living Water would quench my thirst!

But what about my fear of tongues, my dogmatic attitude that it wasn't anything I needed, even the feeling of condescension toward those who did speak in tongues?

All during the conditioning process, the Lord was showing me myself, not only those sins in my life that needed to be confessed and cleansed, along with attitudes that needed to be changed, but apart from these, I was becoming acquainted with the real me. I gained new understanding of my personality and temperament, the reason inward tensions built up, and why so often situations left me locked up inside. God wasn't dealing with my doctrine or theology. He was dealing with specifics, specifically me.

It wasn't until God had stripped me of every excuse, taken every crutch, and I was at the end of myself, that I could begin to comprehend how much I needed this manifestation of the Spirit. Before, it had seemed neither practical nor necessary.

For the time, I wasn't concerned with the scope of application. I was made so aware of my own personal need, not just for blessing, but to engender spiritual wholeness and balance and an outflow ministry.

One thing in particular stood out concerning my need. Whenever confronted by a complex problem, I couldn't let go of it, hashing it over and over in my thinking. I had to have an answer. But the answer was far too often contingent on my mental calisthenics, even when the problem was spiritual. And prayer and praise came out of "my understanding," whether I really understood what God wanted or not.

I began to sense that for me to be released from this pressure, the Lord would have to bypass my mind, to deal directly with my spirit. Praying in the Spirit would certainly be to this end. Would not then this flow of the Spirit bring liberation, release of tensions? I could never know pure unadulterated communication with God until the Holy Spirit gave utterance through song, worship, praise, and prayer!

I saw that without this vertical outflow of my spirit to God, there would never be any extensive horizontal outflow of His love to others.

It was tremendously exciting to consider. Jesus, through the outpouring of the Holy Spirit, had made way for the glorious reality of being clothed with the very presence of God. Immersed in the Spirit, I would have power and authority and position to accomplish anything Christ led me to do.

And there was nothing to fear. In fact, what I had been afraid of was my protection. Whatever Jesus did within or through me would be kept sacred under the canopy of the Spirit of God, if I remained totally receptive and responsive to God's voice, not because of the initial experience, but as by faith I drank daily from the well of living water. This would be the wellspring from which the love of God would flow in and through me to others, while continuing to purify my heart by faith as long as I continued to drink.

The struggle was over. How could I be sure?

Out of His great heart of love, Jesus said, "Ask, and it shall be given you; seek, and ye shall find; knock, and it shall be opened unto you. For everyone that asketh receiveth; and he that seeketh findeth; and to him that knocketh it shall be opened.

"If a son shall ask bread of any of you that is a father, will he give him a stone? or if he ask a fish, will he for a fish give him a serpent? Or if he shall ask an egg, will he offer him a scorpion? If ye then, being evil, know how to give good gifts unto your children: how much more shall your heavenly Father give the Holy Spirit to them that ask him?" [5]

Now the debris had been cleared away. I had but to ask! To drink!

The water was gushing from the well . . .

"But you, dear friends, must build up your lives ever more strongly upon the foundation of our holy faith, learning to pray in the power and strength of the Holy Spirit." [1]

—Jude

14.

Panic Praying

Sometimes when my children were small they would come to me so extremely upset, sobbing out such garbled sentences, I could hardly make out what was wrong. Whatever I said to them went unheard: I had to get them quiet first. Only then could I find out the cause of their distress and do something about the problem, perhaps from my viewpoint a little thing, but from theirs, mighty big.

In times of distress I've found myself running to the Lord in almost the same hysterical manner. Thrown for a loop by people or seemingly impossible situations, I felt everything spinning out of control. Trying to cope with the problems only resulted in more mix-up. It was then my prayer gushed out, a mumble-jumbled plea for the Lord to do something quick, a frantic attempt to communicate my immediate hurt or needs to Him in what I've come to term "panic praying."

In such agitation of spirit, we can expect about the same ratio of answers·to prayers as a Tibetan spinning his prayer wheel. In more than one way we're spinning our wheels, although we do have some advantage over the Tibetan. God isn't deaf to panic praying; He doesn't ignore it, and He understands our fears and frustrations.

But frankly, I've learned not to expect to hear His Voice until I become quiet on the inside.

Patiently He waits, while seeking to establish faith and quietness within.

Sometimes I realize my spiritual hysterics at the onset. And when I do, my prayer changes immediately. I ask only, "Lord, quiet my heart before Thee."

If a place of prayer becomes an altar, the kitchen sink is so hallowed by this mother. One day, very much disturbed, I was frantically praying while washing dishes in tears and soapsuds. Suddenly the words, "panic praying," charged into my stirred-up thoughts. Right then I stopped. I repeated the words, *panic praying.* I thought back.

"Yes, Lord, that has been the tempo of most of my praying for a long time now. But why?

"Because I'm looking at all the problems, rather than at *the all-sufficient One!*" The Lord always lets me answer my own *stupid* questions.

Our spiritual honesty enables the Holy Spirit to adjust spiritual perception into sharper focus. The experience is quite comparable to that of gazing down into the Grand Canyon and exclaiming over the fabulous view; then, after dropping a coin in a slot (it costs) and looking through the mounted high-powered binoculars, one gets a close-up view and is inadvertently arrested by discoveries not detectable before.

In the same way, frankly admitting the reason for my panic praying made possible the enlarging of my scope of understanding, the Holy Spirit causing me to see beyond what I already knew. It wasn't only that I'd become obsessed with the seemingly impossible situation, but panic praying had been my reaction when I'd failed to see God working in the midst of the muddle. I'd spent a lot of time bemoaning "the wrongs." God didn't seem to be doing anything about any of them; things were apparently getting worse not better.

His Lordship even in this? Absolutely!

Confidence that the Lordship of Jesus Christ stands over every situation I've utterly relinquished to Him, doesn't depend on the apparent. What I saw or didn't see God doing was entirely irrelevant. Jesus Christ was my Lord; He was in absolute control.

Panic praying comes out of confusion as opposed to confidence. Give the devil credit for what is happening and he pays off promptly, meting out confusion. Confidence is the gift of God. "For God did not give us a spirit of timidity—of cowardice, of craven and cringing and fawning fear—but [He has given us a spirit] of power and of love and of calm and well-balanced mind and discipline and self-control." [2]

Why? That we might come to the Lord as He intended, not filled with panic, but ". . . *with thanksgiving* let your requests be made known." [3] Our confidence in His Lordship is our surety of victory, whatever the valley experience.

I have very little, if any, of the phlegmatic in my natural temperament. But I've learned one thing: although by nature I may be as high-strung as a racehorse, God wants me to get quiet on the inside before I concern myself with bringing any other need to Him. Not only is this what God wants, I've found it absolutely essential to any depth of communication with the Father and Son. So this is one of my most frequent prayers: "Quiet my heart before Thee!"

For years I had claimed and quoted, "In quietness and in confidence shall be your strength . . .",[4] but I had more confidence in the Lord, than quietness of spirit. Then I saw: for quietness and confidence to be my strength, quietness must come first!

Confidence in a person comes from knowing him well enough to be assured that he won't let you down in a crisis. Confidence in God comes from that intimate relationship with Jesus whereby we come to know the Father through His Word and through the Holy Spirit. Confidence, like faith, is a gift, but it develops as we experience His faithfulness in our daily walk with the Lord.

But what about quietness? Where and how do we attain that quietness which God says shall in itself be our strength? Certainly responsibility is involved, because "Be still, and know that I am God," [5] is a command. And the word "still" here indicates an attitude of letting alone and ceasing from whatever you are doing.

It was Harold Irish who called one day to share that God had showed him "Be still" even meant "Go to sleep . . . and when you wake up, you'll have the answer."

Samuel was an old grayheaded man when he called all the people together and commanded them to "stand still, that I may reason with you before the Lord of all the righteous acts of the Lord, which he did to you and to your fathers." [6] He is plainly telling them to stay put right in the spot where they are standing, to hush up and keep quiet that they might hear what he has to say. Then he reviews their deliverance from Egypt: points out how often as a nation they had repented when defeated by their enemies only to forget God again once they were safe; their sin in wanting a king to reign over them instead of being content to serve with single allegiance the Lord God who was already their King. He warns of judgment if they continue in wickedness and declares the sovereignty of God in making the Israelites His people, never forsaking them, not because of their righteousness, but for His own Name's sake. Thus as they stand in quietness before Him, Samuel causes them to know God's good and right ways.

But they had to get quiet first.

While we may have trouble identifying with the exploits of many Bible characters chosen of God to be used by Him, most of us can readily identify with their weaknesses. I'm so glad God didn't leave the unsavory out, that the whole account is there. For while rubbing my own spiritual black-and-blue marks, I can read of the Bible "greats" and take heart that they too knew failure and defeat, that they bumped their shins while learning to walk with God in the valley in the dark. It's clear that "panic praying" is no innovation of mine. Some of the Bible greats got into desperate straits, and they sent up quite frantic and panicky prayers.

Jonah tried to flee to Tarshish from the presence of the Lord and ended up in a formidable plight. I'm glad the Lord recorded his prayer. In the second chapter of Jonah, I learn two things: the extreme panic and despair that that preacher knew even as he prayed; also the point of transition in his prayer that brought him release.

Listen to his cry from the belly of the great fish: "When my soul fainted within me I remembered the Lord: and my prayer came in unto thee, into thine holy temple. . . . But I will sacrifice unto thee with the voice of thanksgiving. . . . Salvation is of the Lord!" [7]

Even with the seaweed wrapped around his head, Jonah remembers the Lord. Samuel had rebuked the Israelites for their ingratitude, entreating them to remember the Lord and all the manifestations they had known of His mercy as well as warnings of His judgments. Jonah, remembering, knows he is where he is because of his rebellion and God's ensuing judgment. He also recognizes he is alive only because of God's mercy. Remembering the Lord, he sees his situation as God sees it.

To see as God sees, to understand God's dealings with us—both are big steps toward quietness of heart and liberty of spirit.

I have found the best way to begin to "remember the Lord" is to get alone and saturate myself in the Word, giving careful attention to the basic principles by which God has endeavored to prepare a people for His holy habitation, a temple of living stones for the Living God to dwell therein, encompassing all believers down through generation after generation. Then I consider how I have known the personal application of these principles by the Spirit.

The Lord had prepared the only "prayer closet" of its kind for Jonah, one which didn't even require his shutting the door. But for all the whale blubber which encased him, he knew his prayer had reached the Lord even in his holy temple. Hopeless as his situation seemed, he could still know communication with his Lord, because the inner-communication was within his own spirit.

Sacrifice was offered in the temple: Jonah's sacrifice of praise and thanksgiving was being offered within that habitation of God in his innermost spirit where God dwelt.

One night I received a phone call which left me stunned. Spiritual issues were involved, an irrevocable decision being made which could very well prove disastrous. I was painfully concerned, for ones I loved dearly were involved. When I went to bed, I lay there still numbly asking, "God, is this right?" Although I tried, it didn't seem I had enough direction from the Lord to even know how to pray. I knew sleep would not come as long as my spirit was so disturbed.

It had only been a short time before that the Lord had been able to get through to me how biblical glossolalia could fulfill need in my life. Even though it had been a manifestation of the baptism in the Spirit in the early church, for years I had rejected it, not seeing how praying in tongues could serve any present purpose to the church collectively or to the members individually. Then God brought circumstances to bear which exposed the particular need I had which Jesus wanted to meet in this specific way. Thus it was no longer a choice to be accepted or rejected as I had thought. If Jesus was absolute Lord of my life, my every motive was compellingly tantamount to His desires. He had made plain His desire to impart and for me to receive by faith. There was no alternative of choice.

I was thinking about that phone call, still stunned by its implications. Then I knew the Lord was speaking.

"Do you know why I allowed this to happen and why you've drawn a blank when asking Me whether it is right or wrong? The only prayer you could possibly pray right now, is 'Thy will be done.' And you would only be mouthing words. Do you know why the numbness of spirit?"

I had an inkling. I got up, took my Bible, and slipped into the adjoining bedroom where no one was sleeping. I also took a draft of an article by my friend, the Reverend Bob Mumford, entitled "What Good Is It?" Bob had given it to me a couple of months before when we had attended a conference where he had been teaching. In an unusual way God had brought us together, and then and since, his has been an amazing and deeply appreciated ministry to our family.

Although in a hurry to leave for his plane that morning, he had dashed back up to his room for the article, believing it to contain some of the answers for which he knew I was searching, even though we had not discussed the subject.

I was open to the truth in the article because Bob had created desire in my heart for what he had in God. He was so genuine, with so much zest for living, and a tremendous outflow of God's love. Just as rare and particularly intriguing to me, he made the flow of the Spirit practical to everyday living.

For a long, long while, I had had an increasing awareness that there was a whole new dimension to prayer which I needed to discover for myself. My hurt had intensified that awareness. I didn't understand how it could be, but I felt God had to do something, or I couldn't stand it. However, I knew that whatever He did had to be based on the Bible, or I'd rather stay spiritually anesthetized.

I had gone over the article, the Scripture proofs, many times. But I did it again. Then I turned to the thirty-second chapter of Isaiah. The burden of my need was overwhelming as I sat there on the floor beside the bed talking out my bewilderment to Jesus. I asked for openness of heart and for enlightenment by the Spirit.

It seemed like my whole being was one consuming desire, the desperate need for the Holy Spirit to so penetrate my spirit and being that there would come a divine, supernatural quietness of human spirit. To me, this was the way it would have to be according to Isaiah 32:15, the Spirit outpoured bringing quietness and assurance, letting me relax in God.

There was still so much I didn't understand, and I told the Lord as honestly as I knew how.

"I need Jesus," my heart cried. "I need Jesus right now. I can't go on like this!"

In the weeks and months past, the Lord had been dredging up an awful lot of mud. I'd asked Him not to let me get away with anything, and I meant it. I was determined not to sidestep any of His dealings, painful as they might be.

As I leveled with the Lord that night, I knew I had reached the ground of my heart where I could say in all honesty, "My heart is open to You with no reservations. And I know You have promised to pour out the Holy Spirit from on high . . ."

Knowing that the work of the Spirit is to take the things of Jesus and make them mine, that He does express Himself through the human spirit yielded to Him, I prayed, "If this language of the Spirit which I don't comprehend is tongues, I'm ready. Because I'm trusting the protection of the shed Blood and the canopy of the Holy Spirit, I know I have nothing to fear. I don't care what You do or how You do it—but please pour Your Holy Spirit over, let Him flow in and through, bringing quietness to my spirit . . . and let me be able to worship You as You want to be worshiped."

I had always been afraid of that which might not be real. But now I knew these weeks had been preparing me for this moment, cleansing out the dross, teaching me what real openness and honesty with God meant. Knowing I was being open with the Lord now, I knew I was safe! Jesus would never let anything come to me that was not of Him—if He did, He had more to lose than I, for His Word would be broken.

"Lord," I continued, "I don't even want to pray about the circumstances revealed by that phone call. Only let me worship God as the Spirit gives utterance . . . until my spirit becomes quiet and I can rest. Pour Your Spirit over me . . . let me receive of You . . ."

It was strangely quiet. Suddenly that which for years I had so complicated, became amazingly simple. I had never been able to disconnect in my thinking, the baptism of the Spirit, from some emotion-packed, dramatic episode. Rather, here I was sitting on the floor, leaning back against the bed, eyes open, simply talking quietly with the Lord, when it seemed that faith suddenly took hold. The next moment I began to worship and praise the Lord in that same simple quiet way—but in a new language. At once I knew it to be the language of the Spirit.

As I sat there worshiping, barely above a whisper, I was keenly aware of a strange quietness within and surrounding me. When I was a child, sleeping out in the Cascades or the Olympics in the night, the stillness used to seem so intense it could be felt. So it was when Jesus came into the room that night to meet my need. Such a profound quietness with the preciousness of His Presence! There were no emotional stirrings of exhilaration, there was an absolute void of the dramatic. Nothing but a deep, transcendent, pervading peace of spirit.

After a half hour or so, I went back to bed. Switching on the nitelight, I opened my Bible. My heart was full of wonder. I had to read the words once more: "Until the spirit be poured upon us from on high . . . and the work of righteousness shall be peace; and the effect of righteousness quietness and assurance for ever." I turned back a page. "In quietness and in confidence shall be your strength. . . ." [8] I turned off the light, and for the first time in weeks, almost immediately fell asleep.

The morning following, as I went about my work, I was still wondering at the ease with which I had expressed worship with words I knew did not originate in my mind. It seemed too simple, too natural, to be real. The Lord spoke plainly: "I have filled you with My Spirit. Rejoice and be glad."

But none of what had happened fit any doctrinal pattern or theology I'd been taught.

"What about the experience of the baptism in the Holy Spirit?" I wondered.

Why do we insist on hanging on to man's theology and our own set ideas rather than the Living Word, or just letting God be God, manifesting His Spirit as He will?

But the Lord patiently answered, "I didn't want you to glory in any experience or even be aware of an experience. I simply wanted you to receive, to let Me work in quietness . . ."

"But Lord, I thought surely I would know 'the consummation of the unquenchable flame.' "

"No," came the answer, "because you needed to know that I am also in the still small voice."

How beautifully God adapts Himself to our temperament, our individuality, our specific needs!

As to how it happened, I wrote Bob: "I fell in the river of living water— I didn't make a splash, but I sure came up dripping wet! . . . After having all the answers for so long, it was so void of the dramatic it was almost funny . . ." I've had to chuckle more than once at how the Lord does things in a way to upset our set notions.

I thought then of the rest of Jonah's prayer. He had vowed to sacrifice unto the Lord with the voice of thanksgiving. In Hebrews we are admonished to "offer the sacrifice of praise to God continually, that is, the fruit of our lips giving thanks to his name." [9] While I'd certainly sacrificed sparingly, I knew we are to offer the sacrifice of praise continually—which means praising when I don't feel like it—in English. Would the Lord desire such sacrifice in the language of the Spirit? I began to wonder about many things.

Yes, I still had questions. However, I was already beginning to see a deeper meaning to life in the Spirit; neither the baptism in the Spirit, nor the signs and wonders are ever an end in themselves. If tongues, or any manifestation of the Spirit, continued to fulfill a biblical place in my life, I must realize there would be increased perception and spiritual growth through continued faith and obedience. What I had received was not as a picture to be hung on the wall to be admired. It was as a tool to be used as the Spirit directed.

No, I didn't have all the answers. But I was learning—and learning is a process, not a point of arrival.

Jonah had been taken to the deepest depths in order to learn the meaning of being subject to the Lord. God had taken me through more than one valley experience to teach me to "let" Him be Lord in seemingly impossible situations, in times of bewilderment and hurt. He had been working to bring quietness of spirit and confidence in His perfect control, regardless of whether I saw what He was doing or not. There was no need to resort to panic praying if I remained committed to the absolute Lordship of Jesus Christ and remained open to the continued ministry of the Holy Spirit flowing through me in praise to God.

Jonah's prayer, which started out in panic, reaches a triumphant climax with this testimony of faith: "Salvation is of the Lord!" Jonah's unfeigned declaration of his committal to the Lord in the midst of an impossible situation caused the miracle of his release from the black murkiness of that living submarine.

So we find submission to His Lordship is not a chain that binds, but a power that releases, for no longer are we held captive by self-devotion—our devotion is to Christ and we have found our place in the Kingdom of God. And "of the increase of his government and peace there shall be no end." [10] Try that one on for size!

Any experience God gives us is to bring us into a new way of life, a new dimension of faith. So with the baptism in the Spirit. It is not the initial experience that is the important thing, but what follows.

Whereas, before, I had dwelt in a small room, well-fed, well-provided for in every way, one day I looked through an open door into a field of buried treasure that stretched before me as far as I could see. When I walked through that doorway, there was a fresh breeze of the Spirit blowing, the warm sunlight of God's love, and I was given an instrument that would serve to uncover many rich treasures. But using the instrument would be up to me. I would have to do the digging.

So I see the experience of the baptism in the Spirit as a door opening up to a whole new unexplored territory in the realm of the Spirit. New paths become accessible where we can walk with God, and which lead to a whole new dimension of prayer and faith and love. The flow of the Spirit through the language of the Spirit was the Holy Spirit of God lending Himself to human instrumentality that the riches of God in Christ Jesus might become personally mine.

Shortly after I entered this new territory, God showed me what had happened the moment, by faith, I had stepped across the threshold. I "saw" the huge chain Jesus had broken to set me free. There were four jagged prongs of steel where it had been wrenched in two in the middle of a link. And then as I saw that the two pieces of that broken link were splotched with blood, I heard Jesus say, "With My own hands I broke it—to set you free."

Jesus had broken the chain at its strongest point. Only God and I know the power of that chain—forged of prejudices, religion, orthodoxy, and fears—which had me bound. And how great the release when that chain was broken!

Love had paid a terrible price to set me free. It was because of Calvary that I could receive His total provision to live and walk in the Spirit. To think how long I had struggled against such love!

I cannot ignore the fact that there has always been an inner reluctance in me to be identified with anything "Pentecostal," because the anointing has been misspent by so many who wear that label. And the common tendency is to equate charisma with the "ism," even when there is no link to a denomination.

But in shrinking from the stigma of tongues, I had cheated myself. For through the disciplined exercising of this gift, I have found a greater release of spirit than I ever dreamed possible. I never knew prayer could be like this!

But lest anyone should misunderstand, let me state clearly, "tongues" is not synonymous with "the Holy Spirit." The Holy Spirit is a person. Tongues is only one manifestation of His indwelling the believer.

Sometimes I find myself asking myself, "Is this me? Is this really me!" For life in the Spirit has wrought many remarkable changes.

My prayer life has been utterly transformed. There is the wondrous continual daily intimate communion with Jesus, whether I'm washing dishes, driving the car, working on a manuscript, or whatever. The answers that have come through worship and praise and intercession in the Spirit have been amazing.

And there have been other discoveries. Often when pain is so severe I cannot sleep, or when I'm up-tight from certain pressures, while praying in the Spirit, I will drop off to sleep. The usual pattern would have been a long wakeful night.

Has it always worked this way? Not always have I found release from pain, but always there is a settling of my spirit when there is complete yielding to the Holy Spirit. The flow of the Spirit, in the language He gives, never fails, even through the valley of suffering and pain, to bring a renewed awareness of the presence of the indwelling Christ and the surety of His Lordship standing over all.

I shall always be grateful for John Sherrill's book, *They Speak with Other Tongues*. In it, for the first time, I was confronted with facts apart from hearsay, and God used it to level the first of the barriers.

When speaking of his own experience, Mr. Sherrill uses the phrase, "new-found health." This expresses so well the wholeness that is God's purpose in His ministry to us through the flow of the Spirit—not just physical, but mental, emotional, and spiritual health.

The gifts of the Spirit cannot be separated from the Person of Christ or from the love which He commands. Therefore, through the exercise of the charismatic gifts, the flow of love is in itself a healing force. Both in the initial experience and in the daily use of tongues, there is a sense of being "washed through" by God's love. And I am continually learning how to let His love flow in and through in ministry to others. For the fruit of the Spirit is being produced and perfected as there is the continual response to the voice of the Spirit in worship and service.

I have always loved the Word, but it has come alive in a new way. And I am falling deeper and deeper in love with Jesus as God is answering the prayer of my heart, "that I might know Him!" I am experiencing an enlarging of my concept of God as my Heavenly Father, and of His love.

And through the flow of the Spirit in prayer, there continues that divine operation to establish me in righteousness and stabilize me in God. Whether I stand on the mountaintops or walk through the valleys, there is a King who reigneth. I know. "There is a river, the streams whereof shall make glad the city of God, the holy place of the tabernacles of the most High. God is in the midst of her; she shall not be moved . . ."[11]

Have you drunk from the river of God's love? The flow of the Spirit will turn panic praying into positive, faith-filled, productive prayer. This I know.

> "Fear ye not, stand still, and see the salvation of the Lord. . . . The Lord shall fight for you, and ye shall hold your peace." [1]
>
> —Moses

15.

Faith That Stands Still—in the Valley

Sometimes my dreams have been nightmares in which I have been so terrified I would try to run and find it impossible. I used to wonder if in actuality this would be the case. I rather doubted it, after the night while I was in college when five of us students had a frightening experience and I outran everyone, the fellows included.

However, I do know that when there are spiritual conflicts they can be terrifying, and the most difficult order issued by the Lord is, "Stand still!" He's not just saying, "Don't pick up your feet!"

After the Israelites had fled Egypt and were camped in the wilderness, they looked up to see Pharaoh in hot pursuit. Their first reaction was to wish themselves back in Egypt. But Moses assures them they have nothing to fear, if they will stand still. They shall see the salvation of the Lord. He didn't mean they weren't going anywhere, for his next orders are to pull up their tent pins and get moving!

Standing still, as the Lord directs, has nothing to do with remaining in a certain spot geographically. It is that undisturbed attitude of the heart, of defenseless quietness, trusting God's deliverance and direction.

158

Three million scared Israelites, with the Red Sea ahead and the Egyptians fast closing the gap behind them—and what does Moses say? "Stand still. . . . the Lord shall fight for you, and ye shall hold your peace." [2]
But they are still going through the Red Sea.

Sometimes the enemy catches us unawares, attacking with such force that we are thrown for a loop into spiritual turmoil, our mind thrashing around for the way out of our dilemma, while we feel ourselves slipping from the Rock into the quicksand of fear.

We dare not forget, for the briefest moment, Paul's admonition and warning: "For the weapons of our warfare are not physical [weapons of flesh and blood], but they are mighty before God for the overthrow and destruction of strongholds . . . and we lead every thought and purpose away captive into the obedience of Christ, the Messiah, the Anointed One." [3]

As subjects of the King, our every thought and purpose is to come under His control. Standing still is not a spirit of passivity, but a fixed confidence that causes us to advance according to the Lord's directions without trepidation. Since the battle is His, we need not try to reason a way out when attacked by the enemy, plot our own deliverance, nor fight with the sword of words.

When word came to Jehoshaphat that the enemy was about to swoop down upon Judah, he cried to the Lord: "We have no might against this great company that cometh against us; neither know we what to do: but our eyes are upon thee."

Then upon Jahaziel the Spirit of the Lord came, and he said: "Be not afraid . . . for the battle is not your's [sic] but God's. . . . Ye shall not need to fight in this battle: set yourselves, stand ye still, and see the salvation of the Lord with you." [4]

Set themselves and stand still! Is that what Judah did when they went forth to meet the enemy? No doubt about it. For only the heart that stands still in God, whose eyes are not upon the enemy but upon the Lord, can sing and praise before actually seeing the overthrow and destruction of such a formidable host.

Most of us have our reserve weapons stashed away which we think to use if the Lord doesn't come through. But until we render up all our arms, and our spirit which would seek by any means its own deliverance, concedes to being defenseless, we tie God's hands. He will not fight for me if I retain any confidence in the flesh!

His Lordship! It has to be without reservation. No matter how tightly we are hemmed in, though the strength and strategy of the enemy makes defeat seem inevitable, the Lord wants us to stop trying to manipulate the action, to quit trying to work things out. Neither fight, plot an escape, argue, fret, or be anxious. He wants us to lift our eyes from the threatening peril, to look to Him for victory, to say, "In myself I have no strength . . . but my eyes are upon Thee, Oh, Lord!" [5]

If I have made the Most High God the habitation of my spirit, I can stand still in Him, recognizing any situation as being but another opportunity for the manifestation of the Lordship of Jesus Christ, ever being mindful that He doesn't need the help of human effort, mind, or strength to conquer any foe.

Can you imagine an army spearheaded by a group of singers? So it was with the army of Judah. Jehoshaphat "appointed singers unto the Lord, and that should praise the beauty of holiness, as they went out before the army, and to say, Praise the Lord; for his mercy endureth for ever." [6]

This beautiful act of faith released the power of God in their behalf and wrought such a victory for Judah that they "were three days in gathering of the spoil, it was so much." Even so, we will never find a more potent defense than to sing, praise, and worship —whatever besets us.

Consider that exactly the same Greek word, *nikaō*, is used to describe the triumph of the believer in Rom. 8:37—"In all these things we are *more than conquerors* through him that loved us"— as is used to describe the ultimate triumph of Christ in Rev. 6:2.— "a crown was given unto him: and he went forth *conquering*, and *to conquer.*" Elsewhere in Scripture, the word is translated *overcame* or *overcometh*. But either way, *nikao* leaves no question of total victory.

More than conquerors over what? Paul lists them: suffering, affliction, tribulation, calamity, distress, persecution, hunger, destitution, peril, and the sword. Not later. But *in* all these things.

We don't need to walk out of the valleys to be more than conquerors. We stand in Christ, in every valley—conquerors—regardless of the situation, of anything, of anybody.

Because of this confidence, "I am persuaded, that neither death, nor life, nor angels, nor principalities, nor powers, nor things present, nor things to come, nor height nor depth, nor any other creature, shall be able to separate us from the love of God, which is in Christ Jesus OUR LORD!" [7]

His provision for victory *"in* all these things," was secured by His love. My claim—and the only claim I have—to such transcendent victory, is my position *in Christ*, a position assured by my full recognition, submission, and utter dependence upon the indwelling Christ.

To "stand still, and see" is to *live in God*. What safer place then to abide than in the One who said, "I have overcome the world.—I have deprived it of power to harm, have conquered it [for you]." [8]

As long as we are conscious of any inner struggle against the known will of God, we are not standing still; we are seeking our own way out. If there have been angry words, the clashing of personalities, that disposition to withdraw ourselves from an individual or a group, we are acting and reacting out of fear, not trust toward God nor love and compassion. Though we may recognize our inability to cope with a situation, we want the Lord to make us able, rather than standing still and trusting Him to work the situation out to His glory.

When the enemy attacks in any of these ways, and our minds are taken up trying to figure out all the angles, all the "what if's?" such mental activity saps our spiritual energy to praise and worship, and thus we are disarmed for spiritual warfare.

When we find it difficult to stand still, it is because we are more acutely sensitive to our human senses than we are sensitive to the person of Jesus Christ and His presence. When situations or circumstances become unpredictable we tend to lose our security. Judging by what our eyes see, our ears hear, and our mind tells us, we panic with fear.

Until we take our eyes off the circumstances and leave the future entirely in God's hands, we will know nothing but continued defeat.

But when there is an attitude of meekness, when we acknowledge our utter dependence upon Jesus, when we say, "I cannot see. I cannot understand, but I choose to trust," something happens within. Heart, soul, spirit, body, mind, emotions—all that I am—rise to that "access by faith into this grace wherein we stand, and rejoice in hope of the glory of God." [9]

Have you thought things as they are just now, more than you can endure? Have you been frightened, depressed, given over to despair? Have you thought to escape, by one way or another? Is there seemingly no one to whom you may turn? Have you tried to fight the battles of life in your own strength, or even asked God to help you as you tried one maneuver after another to bring order out of chaos, victory out of defeat?

God wants you to stop trying to be your own salvation. He wants you to stop trying to be other people's salvation. He wants you to stand!

We have stood so many times at closed doors, waiting. Nothing is a greater test of our trust in God.

One such time was, we knew, a point of crisis for our family. A major move was involved. There had been much prayer and seeking God's direction, as it was one of the most difficult decisions of this nature we had ever faced. But just when it seemed God was opening a certain door, it was suddenly locked. For the time clock to release the lock, several things would have to by synchronized. But they weren't. There was nothing to do but wait.

Some weeks passed, but all the while there was no less feeling that this was God's move for us. After a time, it seemed certain steps should be taken in the direction we believed to be God's will.

Then the question came to me: If we were to do so, would we be pushing open a door God had closed?

Of one thing I am certain: I don't ever want to enter a door I've pushed open.

I was determined to stand still while seeking God's answer. The more I prayed, the more I was able to say with certainty that God was pressing us into an immediate move. I knew I had turned the whole thing over to Him. I also knew there were doors which only He could open. And so He did. In perfect timing.

Although it was not without hurt, there was no question when the time came that we were to move and move immediately. We had only marched around the city. God had flattened the walls.

We had scarcely settled in our new location when we received some startling news. A severe windstorm had demolished the mobile home in which we had been living during the past two-and-a-half years.

Because moving did incur deep hurts, the Lord knew we needed to be faced with what seemed impossible. Then when the Lord overcame the impossible and the door swung open, we could keep right on "standing still" on the inside, in the midst of the hurts, because we knew beyond any doubt we were moving in God.

I have never found it otherwise. If a call is really of God, He goes before, and He will give ample confirmation.

When Dr. Phillips Brooks, pacing his study like a caged lion, was asked what was the trouble, he replied, "The trouble? I'm in a hurry, and God isn't! That's the trouble."

How often that is our trouble. We are frustrated when God doesn't rush to our distress, when the answer doesn't appear instantly. But God doesn't need to rush into any situation, for it hasn't caught Him by surprise.

Someone has said, "To 'stand still' takes a mighty faith." That is true principally because we can't separate faith from locomotion.

We even try to convince ourselves that doing something, even if it is wrong, is better than doing nothing. So we have a lot of commotion going on under the misnomer of "faith in action," or "Christian service," or "working for God," when all it really amounts to is religious activity.

Religious activity may stir up a lot of dust. It may build man's kingdom. But it will never build God's Kingdom.

We don't need to stumble around, our footing unsure, trying to do God's will, plotting, finagling, struggling . . . We can stand in Christ, knowing we will see the salvation of the Lord, but not without first rendering up our arms, having no confidence in self, and turning from the opposition affronting us, to fix our eyes upon the Lord, our confidence in Him.

The ability to hold steady under pressure comes from knowing what God has said, and the certainty that God speaks Truth.

When Paul, along with other prisoners, was being transported by boat to Rome, it seemed certain that the voyage would end in tragedy. How could they possibly survive the force of such a hurricane? But Paul said, "I believe God, that it shall be even as it was told me." [10] He was not merely controlling his panic, he was confident God would keep His Word. And so he was content to stay in the boat; why, he was able, in the midst of the storm, to break bread and give thanks.

Victory is without preference. But it is not without being fully persuaded, that "all the promises of God in him are yea, and in him Amen, unto the glory of God by us." [11]

Once we know what God has said, we can sit still and wait—and sing praises!

"For the sake of your tradition . . . you have set aside the Word of God—depriving it of force and authority and making it of no effect. You pretenders—hypocrites!" [1]

—*Jesus*

16.

Bringing Us into Balance

There is something about watching old buildings being razed to make way for the new which engenders in me a ripple of melancholy and emptiness. Somewhat similar is the sensation when God begins His work in us to make all things new.

Before God can build His Kingdom within us, He must of necessity raze that structure which is the expression of man's kingdom, fabricated of pious philosophy, conscientious conduct, legality or liberalism, those meaningless mores. Because we become so comfortable with that with which we are familiar, when the old religious structure begins to crumble, the bereft feeling which follows is frightening. We may even panic. But surely, as the whole comes tumbling down and we find ourselves in the valley of trepidation, we must ascertain what God is trying to do.

When it happens to you and you are gazing at the pile of religious rubble around your feet, you are in one of the lowest low points in all your life. The more religious you have been, the more devastating the feeling. You will probably moan, "But I was such a long time in building . . ." And if you listen, you will most likely hear the Lord say, "How well I know!"

165

A monstrosity, absurd and weird, is the Winchester house near San Jose, California, with its labyrinth of rooms, stairways that lead nowhere, doors which open to nothing but a solid wall. Quite like it are the religious structures man fabricates when building his kingdom—a labyrinth of philosophical ideas, doctrines, and dogmas which deceivingly lead nowhere, solid walls of prejudice which shut one into the narrow confines of self and restrict one from entering into the infinity of God's Kingdom.

Before we have come into that place in God where we have true spiritual discernment, we are prone to take for granted as truth whatever we hear which seems right and good. It may or may not be. Even so, we pick up so much, tacking it together at random, and so we build.

But when God begins building His Kingdom, He will shake the religious edifice we have built, and all that has not been built by the Master Craftsman has to come down. Then comes the discovery: what we thought was a monument of our faith is nothing more than a religious mausoleum.

God's purpose in destroying the old is that He might bring us into spiritual balance. You need to know what God's purpose is lest you be devastated by the demolition process.

The doctrines of God are beautifully balanced. But when a truth has been very meaningful, some would begin to build everything upon that doctrine, and the result is a lopsided structure.

I have been with groups which lay such stress upon man's responsibility that one hardly dared mention the sovereignty of God. On the other hand, some groups contend that man is not liable in any way for what he is, since God's sovereignty leaves him no power of choice.

Those who hold this latter view remind me of the young Moslem I talked with in the hospital. He had been severely burned when an oil freighter caught fire and sank. He talked to me of many things —of the difference between his culture and that of the western hemisphere, of marriage and divorce. To him it seemed incredible that a man grown tired of a marriage relationship should not simply be free to take another wife as he desired. But whatever we talked about, his views were all modified by a cursory shrug and the Islamic sentiment, "If Allah wills . . ." Thereby he thought to abrogate the moral responsibility of man.

But the sovereignty of God and man's moral responsibility are beautifully blended and perfectly balance each other. I like the way one minister puts it: "My rest in the sovereignty of God is in knowing that my obedience to God will cause Him to rule and overrule to accomplish His will in and through me."

The sovereignty of God is one of the believer's greatest sources of security. There have been situations I could never have survived had I not believed explicitly that God held all things in His hand. Nor would I dare to face the tomorrows.

But I have discovered one cannot begin to apprehend nor appreciate the scope and meaning of God's sovereignty until he understands its correlation with moral responsibility. Instead of one truth being sacrificed to the hurt of the other, when they are brought into proper balance, they perfectly complement each other.

It is not that God has all power to accomplish His purposes totally independent of man's doings which makes the sovereignty of God so stupendous, but rather that He dares to delegate authority to man, to use the free moral choices of man, to let man be a self-determined part of what He is doing—and yet He is in no danger of failing to accomplish His eternal purpose.

Perhaps another of the most common doctrines to be overbuilt is that which has to do with death to self. Discovering the proper balance between death to self and life in the Spirit is imperative if one is not to become hopelessly frustrated.

God allows us to go through drastic experiences that we may know daily identification with the Cross as it cuts across our personal rights and desires. However, when God thus begins to reveal ourselves to ourselves, we begin to see so much that needs to be put to death, that we are apt to envision a goal that is not what God intended at all.

That I can reckon myself dead to sin because Christ's death both *for* me and *as* me, not only paid the penalty of my sin, but broke the power of cancelled sin, was a doctrine I eagerly embraced. Even so, certain things proved I was still a very lively corpse. It was most disconcerting.

After I found myself over and over again in the valley of depression, because not by the widest stretch of the imagination did this very real doctrine describe me, the Lord began to show me what the problem was. I had been expecting God to make me into a person void of all normal emotional response. Surely, I thought, if I were truly "crucified with Christ," [2] then I would never know discouragement, fear, distress.

Though the truth I had embraced was as solid as could be, I had become spiritually unbalanced.

Balance began to be restored through a very bitter experience— my discovery that utterly false accusations had been widely circulated about me. I was hurt deeply. Reckoning myself dead to sin didn't stop the tears, nor the ache. God had something to teach me!

The emotions with which I had been created were not sinful, nor were they to be considered disparagingly. God had no desire to make me insensitive to either pleasurable or unpleasurable feelings.

That which made me realize how heavily lopsided this doctrine had become in my thinking was Paul's autobiography. Herein I discovered Paul ran the gauntlet of human emotions. Here is a portion of his testimony.

"We are troubled . . . distressed . . . perplexed . . . cast down." (II Cor. 4:8, 9) . . . in weariness and painfulness . . . in hunger and thirst (II Cor. 11:27). I had no rest in my spirit (II Cor. 2:13). I was with you in weakness, and in fear, and in much trembling (I Cor. 2:3). We were pressed out of measure, above strength, insomuch that we despaired even of life" (II Cor. 1:8).

And there was much more which I found in common with Paul as he went through the valleys.

But the one Scripture which held even greater meaning to me was what Paul said about Jesus. "For though he was crucified through weakness, yet he liveth by the power of God. For we also are weak in him, but we shall live with him by the power of God toward you." [3]

Though we are weak in ourselves, the operation of God's power in our lives enables us to show forth Christ in our relationships with others. There is a tremendous release of spirit when we see ourselves as nothing, when we live, reckoning ourselves dead indeed unto sin. But unless there is the balancing factor of the reality of the life of Jesus Christ surging through, His strength overruling weakness, His love flowing out in every relationship—because of the power of the indwelling Spirit—all of life will add up to one big zero. If we apply the message of the Cross without knowing the reality of the resurrection Life of Jesus Christ, we are miserably out of balance.

Now when I come to comprehend some aspect of truth for the first time, I'm determined to find out also, what is the balancing factor. It is always to be found, either in doctrine or experience or both.

Another part of the religious structure to be razed when we submit to the Lordship of Christ, are the religious practices of man's kingdom. When Jesus as King begins to build His Kingdom within us, He will dethrone all the religious idols which have long controlled our behavior. Until God reveals these idols as such, we never recognize them for what they are.

We accumulate so much false in the traditions of men and continue its perpetration as truth. Many of these traditions have every bit as much sway over our spiritual conduct as idols of wood and stone do over those who worship them.

Whether it be a person, a doctrine, a tradition, to which you give obeisance, God will smash that idol, and you will find yourself every bit as unstrung as the heathen who finds his idol broken, his fetish destroyed.

Rest assured, God will never undermine nor topple the tenets of true faith. But if you yield yourself to the establishing of His Kingdom within, He is going to bring to dust those traditions you have tenaciously held to be spiritual but which are actually a bondage.

I listened to a minister who was also an active psychology counselor in a large public school system, tell how for years he had attempted to press the young people of his denomination into a narrow mold the church had demanded they fit into. "Finally," he said, "I had to admit the Bible didn't set the standards we were demanding of these young people. They were nothing more than the traditions of man." When he refused to be bound any longer, he found a rich and spiritual ministry to both young and old that ministered life and release of spirit.

People find a false security in tradition, for they don't have to search out God for themselves and assume the responsibility of deciding what is God's standard of righteousness, stripped of man's appositions and suppositions. More often than not, our bondage to tradition is much greater to the man who has held these practices to be ordained of God, than to the practices themselves. But as we come under the authority of King Jesus, daily yielding ourselves to righteousness, He will break the diabolic power of mere religious exercises.

While we ourselves will be broken in the valley of broken idols, one thing, and only one thing, will remain undisturbed—that which is genuine about our faith in Jesus Christ. And if we cooperate with the Master Builder, He will begin to build upon that faith.

Notice the prophetic word of Jeremiah: "The Lord hath appeared of old unto me, saying, 'Yea, I have loved thee with an everlasting love: therefore with lovingkindness have I drawn thee. Again I will build thee, and thou shalt be built, O virgin of Israel . . . And it shall come to pass, that like as I have watched over them, to pluck up, and to break down, and to throw down, and to destroy, and to afflict; so will I watch over them, to build, and to plant, saith the Lord." [4]

If you have made Jesus Christ Lord of your life, and have committed yourself to seeking first His Kingdom of righteousness, no doubt God has begun to shake all that can be shaken. But it is no time to run around trying to prop up the building. He is determined to destroy your religion, the lopsided edifice that has been structured by you. Because of His everlasting love will He do this.

But be assured that as you submit yourself to the dealings of God, He will bring to birth that which is spiritual, building the balanced and indestructible Kingdom of the King of Glory within you, O Zion.

"We are not our own bosses to live or die as we ourselves might choose. Living or dying we follow the Lord.
Either way we are his." [1]

—*Paul*

17.

Healing?—in the Valley

I am appalled at some of the remarks preachers make from the pulpit concerning physical illness and faith healing as they relate to a
Christian. Likewise, many books, supposedly written to inspire
faith, cause me to cringe at statements so caustic they would surely
hurt more than they would minister healing. It is tragic but true;
the valley of physical suffering for the Christian is often gouged
deeper by the "healing specialists" in the church.

I'm not referring to those with a genuine Spirit-anointed ministry of healing, for they are imbued with compassion and love and
empathy, as Jesus Christ is manifest through them. But the Christian who is physically afflicted is a prime target for the super-
spiritual with their self-opinionated formulas and pat answers. Believe me, I know!

If you have read this far, you know that I do understand something of physical suffering. And you must know that if I had not
personally experienced God's power to heal, I would not be sitting
here at my typewriter today.

Experience has taught me that God heals in many ways. I have
personally known miraculous instantaneous healing. But I have

known just as great a miracle in God's restoration process. I have had hemorrhages stop immediately in answer to prayer, even though the disease which caused them was not eliminated. I have known divine strength supplied only at the moment of need. I've also known what it is to be desperately ill, and there be no apparent divine intervention to restore health, though many prayed.

But in each instance there was one thing of which I was sure, one thing of which I am always confident: it was and is God who gives me breath and life.

Let me share with you an experience I had many years ago.[2]

"Lord, You can't take my life!" I knew I was dying, but I pleaded desperately with God to let me live.

I was twenty-one. Al and I had been married fourteen months. There was so much of life to be lived yet, so many ambitions to carry out, so many dreams to be fulfilled. I didn't want to die! I wanted to live!

But I *was* dying, and I knew it.

"Al needs me. If You take my life, I'm afraid he'll go off the deep end!" I argued with the Lord.

I'll admit I wasn't placing much faith in either the Lord's power to keep or in my husband's spiritual stability. And I certainly had a distorted idea of my own importance.

But Al had had some rough growing-up years. And then after three years in the army, during World War II, he had come home, his nerves shot.

Truly God had kept His hand on Al's life in a marvelous way. I knew he was a Christian, but he had known so many heartaches and so much suffering, I couldn't leave him alone.

I loved him very much. More, I am afraid, than I loved Christ. And because God is a jealous God, and because of His faithfulness, He took me deep through the valley of the shadow, until I had not only surrendered *my* life but my husband's life to Him—placing us both completely in God's hands and taking my hands off.

It had all happened so fast. It was late September, 1946. I had spent the day at my mother's, sewing. Late in the afternoon I had developed a dull backache. But having known very few really well days in my life, I thought little of it, and went home in time to prepare our evening meal.

Shortly after dinner, I was seized with terrific pain.

"Sounds like kidney stones. Get her to the hospital at once. I'll meet you there," the doctor instructed, after my husband described my symptoms over the phone.

On the way to the hospital, I was seized with a strange premonition that for me this was the end. Since I had spent time and time again in the hospital, hospitalization was no novelty to me, but never had I known such fear.

"I want to go home," I sobbed, as my husband held me close. He had never seen me like that before, and he couldn't understand it.

The next days were a nightmare of pain. At the hospital, treatment was started at once. Initial X ray did not show the location of the stone, and I was too ill for further work-up. Large doses of analgesics did little to ease the pain.

There were no rooms available, and I spent the first night in the hall. Shut in alone behind the green-curtained screens, in spite of the suffering, I felt a single line pulsating through my mind.

Over and over I repeated, "Oh, I am so happy in Jesus." Vainly I tried to remember the rest of the song. How close His presence was! I could not see Him, but I felt as though I could have reached out and touched Him.

In the morning I was moved to a two-bed ward. I am sure God picked my roommate. She was a student nurse whose home was out of state. She was operated on for appendicitis that day.

Later she told me her mother had died when she was born, that her stepmother was a wonderful Christian and had always been very good to her. "But I told her I would never call her Mother or accept her as such." Headstrong and rebellious, she seemed to resent her stepmother's Christian standards and ideals.

The hospital had contacted the girl's parents, and the stepmother arrived the following day. She was a sweet person, but I was quickly aware of the tenseness between the two. They treated each other like polite strangers.

About the fourth day, the pain had somewhat abated, but I was still desperately ill.

One evening when I attempted to read my Bible, my roommate asked timidly if I would read aloud. I scarcely felt able, but was determined to try, since she had shown this interest in God's Word. He gave me strength, and I was able to read a few verses.

On Sunday, the Rev. R. L. Pickett, retired minister of the church in Arlington, Washington, where my husband and I had attended church as youngsters, sat at the breakfast table.

His wife turned and said, "Robert, the Lord awakened me in the night and told me we should go to Everett today and pray for Florence."

"Why, you stole my thunder. I was just going to tell you the same thing," he replied.

My mother-in-law also lived in Arlington, so that afternoon the three of them drove the eighteen miles to Everett, where I was a patient in the General Hospital. As I had been so ill, they stayed only a few minutes, had prayer, and left. Almost immediately I became worse. Much worse!

I do not remember much of the events of the next few days. And then I lapsed into a coma and I do not remember anything.

One morning my mother met the doctor coming out of my room. "How is she this morning?" she asked.

The doctor just shook his head. "Too sick," he said, "and we don't know why. You had better call her husband and her father right away."

Before she went to phone, Mother came into my room. She said I looked as though death had already set in. Being a minister's wife, she had seen enough of death to recognize its presence.

My aunt stopped by, and she and mother tried to rouse me, but I was beyond knowing.

Just as my aunt was leaving, the Rev. J. Franklin Fisher, pastor of the church we attended in Everett, entered the room.

I had been a friend of the Fisher family for several years. Mother said he seemed shocked to see me in such a condition. Of course I did not recognize him either.

He stood at the foot of my bed and quietly prayed. That prayer was the first thing I was aware of hearing since I had become unconscious. I did not connect it with a person; I was simply conscious of it. Then Pastor Fisher left.

Inexplicably, Mother did not go at once to place the phone call, twice interrupted.

Scarcely fifteen minutes had passed when I opened my eyes, and sat up in bed. Mother said I looked as though I were awakened from a deep sleep.

"I guess the Lord is going to let me live after all," I smiled weakly, and then added, "I would like some tomato juice with lemon in it." Strangely, I had never cared for it before!

I was being fed intravenously and had not been allowed even a drop of water by mouth. My temperature had been hovering at 106.

When Mother asked a nurse's aide for the tomato juice I had requested, the aide replied, "I'll ask the supervisor, but Mrs. Bulle is under strict orders to receive nothing by mouth."

It seemed the answer was that since I was not expected to live through the day, I could have whatever I wanted. I doubt whether this procedure is ethical, but God knew what my system needed. They brought the juice to me. I drank it with no ill effects.

In the meantime, when I had suddenly sat up in bed and announced that I believed the Lord was going to let me live, my roommate had burst out crying, "Oh, pray for me, pray for me!" She held out her arms to her stepmother sitting across the room. "Oh, Mother, Mother," she sobbed, "forgive me, forgive me." Instantly they were locked in each others' arms, and the rest of their words were for their ears alone.

Soon a nurse came and took my temperature. It was normal. Another nurse came and took it again. It was still normal. Then the supervisor and several nurses came in and stood at the foot of my bed, just staring at me and shaking their heads in unbelief.

I was weak, of course, and had to gain my strength back, but in a couple of days I was up and home again.

But there is more to the story than this. While I was in the coma, I was unconscious to the things about me, but I was in the presence of God, and He told me many things.

I did not understand that He did not want to take my life then, but He did want my will to be completely surrendered to His will.

"Lovest thou me?"

"I love You, Lord, but I love Al too . . . and he needs me," I argued.

"Don't you think that a God who made the universe in its matchless wonder, and created man in the first place, is able to watch over him if I take you Home?"

Oh, how glibly we say that we have placed all on the altar, but when a real test comes we realize how incomplete is our consecration.

Finally came full surrender—and peace. At the moment I had said, "Yes, Lord, I am willing to be taken, if that is Thy will," He had restored my life through a miracle.

I was to learn later that at the same time, the Lord had been dealing with my husband about a certain matter. The time of my healing coincided almost exactly to the time he too said yes to God's will.

All this happened over twenty years ago, and I have never had a recurrence of kidney stones. Medically, this is considered remarkable. However, since I was fourteen, I have been afflicted with a serious, chronic lung disease. Even though God has raised me up again and again, in this there has not been complete healing.

When I had reached a very low point, a few years ago, I was set upon by several well-meaning individuals to believe God for a miracle of healing. They were positive this was God's will for me, and adamant in what they considered Scripture proof.

While I appreciated their concern, either they were mistaken or I wasn't getting the message. I tried to explain that I did know the miracle of instantaneous healing when at the point of death, but that somehow I felt this was not to be God's way at this time. He had something else for me now, something more important than physical healing was taking place in the dealings of God in my life. I was willing to trust Him completely. What all was involved, I didn't know. But I did know that it had to be desperately important for the Lord to let me go through all of this. As I continued to get worse, I was aware of spiritual eyebrows being raised at my apparent lack of faith. Yet deep within, there was a sense of God in control that there were not words to express.

But now there came a darker valley, discouragement, depression, despair. And yet, beneath the turbulent surface, there was a depth of trust which remained undisturbed. Then when things looked the blackest, there came a turning point: He touched me!

I had been sick all that year, in and out of the hospital. My last fifteen days in the hospital had meant missing our son Steve's high school baccalaureate and commencement. And then on a Sunday I had come home, knowing that I couldn't keep going on like this; it could only be a matter of time.

A longtime missionary friend, home from Argentina for a brief stay, invited us to a summer camp meeting where he would be a speaker. When I mentioned to one of my doctors that I would like to go but I didn't know whether I could even stand the 280-mile drive or not, he encouraged me, saying, "If anybody does anything for you, God is going to have to do it."

On the following Saturday, we drove to where the camp was already in progress. A bed in our station wagon made it possible. And though I was very weak, there was something stirring within, an expectancy that this was the place God was going to meet my need.

On Sunday, in the afternoon service, the first of several striking incidents occurred. At the close of the meeting, the minister in charge asked our missionary friend who was the man sitting beside him. Was he a minister? He asked to be introduced after the benediction to "the man" who was my husband.

As they met, tears came to the minister's eyes, as he said, "Sir, I've never seen you before. I don't know your name nor who you are. But since a half-hour before this service ended, I have had such a burden for you for deliverance and intercession. Tell me, are you having problems?"

My husband answered quickly. "Are we ever having problems!"

In the few minutes they talked together, an appointment was set up for the following Tuesday. He asked my husband to bring me along to his office.

Though his ministry had been extensive, the Sunday evening speaker was a man whose name I had not even heard. Since he did not arrive until time for the evening service, the first time I ever saw him was when he walked onto the platform after the meeting had already started. He couldn't have known anything about me, yet that sermon remains unforgettable; it couldn't have been more applicable: "The Four Escapes of Life"—and one of them was giving up the will to live.

Having been so very sick and on such heavy medication, at times I found it difficult to think clearly; but now, about three-fourths of the way through the message, in one frightening moment, my mind spun into utter confusion while I was swept through with a terrible feeling of desolation. In that same instant, I realized the speaker had stopped, his words left hanging in mid-air. Quickly his eyes moved over the crowd to look directly at me. He smiled, and in that smile, something of Jesus flowed from him to me. No bolts of electricity, no "feeling the power." It was far deeper than the physical, and yet all my senses were intensely aware of the flow, of something supernatural happening. It was as though I was literally wrapped in compassion.

My mind cleared instantly. (Afterward, he told me that he had felt this huge wave of compassion rolling within, and then as it were, rolling from him. He knew exactly where it settled. And when he looked down at me, he had seen a thousand things and he had seen death. I thought of Jesus saying that when the woman touched the hem of His garment, He perceived virtue had gone out from Him.) No one but the two of us even knew what had happened. What I felt was the presence of Jesus and the overwhelming reassurance of God's love. I needed it then, and it would serve to hold me steady in that which lay ahead.

The message was over, the crowd was standing with bowed heads, singing, when he slipped quietly down the aisle, through to where I was sitting. I felt his hand on my head, heard him praying, and the one phrase is cut deeply into my memory: "Death has already set in . . ." Cursing "death" in the name of Jesus, he asked God to do a work of restoration.

Then he was back in the pulpit, the benediction given, the people dismissed, and it had all happened so unobtrusively, so swiftly, that most were not even aware of what had taken place.

As the auditorium emptied, he motioned me to remain seated. I couldn't have moved anyhow. In a few minutes he came back down and sat beside me. What was the matter, and did I know that time was running out fast? Yes, I well knew! Briefly I told him how desperate was the whole situation.

It's hard to describe my feelings other than that I was somewhat numbed by what was happening. Telling him what had taken place in the afternoon service with my husband, I blurted out, "What is God trying to do?" It was frightening. To think that out of all the hundreds of needs represented in that packed-out auditorium, Jesus, through His servant, had laid His hand on me. I was staggered by the sovereignty of God and His love so manifest, while deep within, my heart was crying: "Who am I, Lord? Who am I?"

It was agreed that we would meet together on Tuesday morning. As it worked out, my husband and I spent several hours together and separately with these two ministers. The Holy Spirit so remarkably revealed our need, made them aware of specific problems. Such ministry could only have been born of God.

Wednesday afternoon I had to go to the hospital for emergency-room treatment. From then on, I spent most of the time in bed, except that I was able to attend the evening services. God was saying so much.

One afternoon, as the minister who had been particularly burdened for me talked with me, he told me he felt strongly that God was not going to do an instantaneous work of healing this time. I answered that I knew this already. He also believed God had begun a restoration process; it would take time, and I was not to get impatient with myself. I was going to need to remember!

A couple of weeks later when I went back to my doctor, my blood pressure was normal for the first time in several months. He pulled up a stool and smilingly asked, "Well, what happened?"

Two weeks after that I was checked by my other doctor. When he read the report from the emergency room, he exclaimed, "What were you doing up there!"

I smiled easily. "Oh, I went to a Bible conference."

He said nothing, but I could almost hear what he was thinking. After the examination, I said, "Dr.——, maybe much doesn't show on the outside yet, but God has done a miracle on the inside—the turmoil's gone."

He looked down at me and then pointed up. "HE had to do it," he said. "You were so far down, there was no other way but up."

Everything the Lord did during those days at camp was tested in the weeks following. Only two weeks after we arrived home, Daryl, our sixteen-year-old son, was nearly killed when the car he was driving hit a tree. The Lord gave the needed strength, and I was able to care for him. In every other crisis too, and there were many that year, the Lord provided all that I needed to see me through.

However, while I was much better in many ways, severe pain was still a problem. And I was still taking at least seven different medications a day. Since pain seemed to provoke conflict in the family, my method of avoiding conflict was to load up on tranquilizers and pain pills, all the time knowing that it wasn't God's way. The doctor worried, saying I was on far too much medication, but he didn't know what to do about it, I was getting so little sleep as it was.

And then the Lord began that inner nudging to get off the drugs. It seemed impossible!

And it would have been. "But God . . ."

It was the next spring when the minister so used of God to help me the summer before, was speaking a short distance from where we now live. It was the first time we had seen him since then, though we had been in touch by letter.

Though he did know I was on a lot of medication, he did not know what I was taking. While speaking that night, however, he made this statement: "People are on everything these days, LSD, marijuana, librium . . ."

I almost fell off my chair!

For a long time I had been on heavy doses of librium or valium, essentially the same. It hardly seemed a drug which a person would mention offhand.

Later I asked, "Why did you say *librium?*"

He said, "I don't know. As far as I know, I've never mentioned it before when I've been preaching."

What else, but that I was being confronted by God!

Sensing the fear that was beginning to build up inside, he said, "God is evidently trying to take your crutches. But you mustn't feel that God has pulled the rug out from under you, nor should you feel guilty. I don't believe you can stop everything at once. But perhaps you can start cutting back . . ."

He then prayed that the Lord would give wisdom, that I would know exactly what to do.

Even then, I knew that for me there was only one way. Stop it all, as of that hour.

The ten days that followed were without parallel to any others I have known, as my body and emotions battled the withdrawal symptoms. But the Lord gave me some very definite instructions. I was just to rest, not try to push myself, drink lots of fruit juice and fluids. And I wasn't to say I would never take any more medicine. Committing myself to any such arbitrary statement would be putting myself right back under bondage. Rather, I was to be sensitive to the Lord's directions, drawing on His imparted Life, taking just one hour at a time.

When a friend who is a nurse expressed concern that in stopping the medications, I should be under "expert supervision," my friend, Jeannie Calder, studied a moment. Then her eyes widened and she pointed up. "What more 'expert supervision' is there?" she laughingly shrugged.

That's Jeannie! But she won't know until now, how God used that to help me through times I nearly panicked.

When the pain became almost a consuming force, it was through the quiet flow of the Spirit, in worship and praise and submission, that I found the greatest release. This in itself has given me a profound sense of the value of tongues in daily devotion. Even in the darkest moments, there would come a deep inner calm, and the security of knowing I was in the hands of the Great Physician, the overwhelming awareness of His love enfolding me. I *was* under "expert supervision."

During this time, another miracle was taking place in our household. As Daryl himself put it, "God finally got through to me how big He was and how little I was." It was the climax of a long struggle over the claims of Christ, and when he was born anew, the change was terrific. But from the time I quit the pills, he constantly encouraged me to trust God. His faith was contagious!

One day when it was the roughest, there came that sudden enlightening of the Spirit which made me apprehend something more of what was happening. There was the communicated assurance that the Lord was not being harsh or demanding in leading me into this valley where I was suffering withdrawal. Then I heard Jesus speak, and it was more than a challenge to faith; it was communication in depth. It was His outpoured love. He said, "In all of this, I'm giving you the opportunity to trust Me."

From that moment on, I could truly give thanks for every second of every twenty-four hours. I never doubted that there would be victory, for I knew the One who died for me was worthy of all my trust.

I would be less than honest if I did not say, yes, there is still pain, sometimes constant, sometimes extreme. But as I am writing this nearly two years later, I can say, God wonderfully set me free— free from the tranquilizers, the pain pills, the sleeping pills. I cannot begin to tell what this means!

However, the greatest thing which God has done, has been that which has been done in my spirit by the Holy Spirit. It has been a precious time of learning to know God, of developing a more vigorous consciousness of the indwelling Christ, of coming to ascertain the practical ministry of the Spirit. And for the obedience of faith to embrace this confidence, "that He Who began a good work in you will continue until the day of Jesus Christ—right up to the time of His return—developing . . . and perfecting and bringing it to full completion in you." [3]

Today I can say, from personal experience: I know Jesus Christ, the Son of the Living God, is my Healer; more than that, I know He is my life. Beyond this, I refuse to be dogmatic about the doctrines of divine healing.

God will never allow Himself to be restricted by any man's narrow creed or opinionated ideas. The Pharisees tried it, and their descendants are still with us, trying to force doctrinal regimentation.

But you cannot regiment love.

True faith not only believes Christ heals, but has faith in the wisdom of Christ's ways of healing, knowing that His ways are higher than our ways.[4]

Someone has said, "Christ was the Great Adapter, yet the Changeless One. His ways varied as He saw the individual needs; physically, mentally, and spiritually."

It is a fallacy to lift a single case from Scripture and say, this is what you must do to receive healing. Depending upon which case you used as precedent, you could infer some strange conclusions, both erroneous and absurd.

You might point to the multitudes Jesus healed and say, "You have to *come* . . ." To the man blind from birth, and say, "You have to *go* and *wash* . . ." To the woman with the issue of blood, "You have to *touch* . . ." To the nobleman's son, "You have to have *a father with authority.* Or to the Syrophenician woman, and say, "You have to *have a mother who lets the dogs eat under the table.* Or to the man who was let down through the roof, and say, "You must have *four friends with a ladder and a crowbar* . . . who *believe.*" Or to others, and say, "No it has to be *your own faith* . . ."

Jesus didn't say the same thing to everyone to whom He ministered. He met each person at his point of need. There was only one common-to-all focus—Jesus Himself, the Son of God.

.

Whenever I am confronted by someone declaring emphatically, "The Bible says, 'The prayer of faith shall save the sick'!" and they contend that the only possible reason healing has not taken place is lack of faith, I have learned to say, "Yes, the Bible does say that. I know I don't have all the answers. But I do know that love and faith can reach beyond healing to accept God's exceptions."

If you think there are none, think again. According to the Law given to Moses by God, David should have been stoned. But David was God's man to rule as king. If we had been among the congregation, we might have thought to "uphold God's laws" by clamoring for the stoning of David. Yet was not David one of God's exceptions? And how about Ruth, the Moabitess, whose marriage to Boaz put her in the direct Messianic line! And what of Hosea, a prophet of God, under divine orders to take as his wife, a harlot? To me, God's exceptions give us to know that a single flat statement cannot tell the whole picture.

Hebrews, chapter eleven, records the faith of "[men] of whom the world was not worthy, roaming over the desolate places and the mountains, and [living] in caves and caverns and holes of the earth. And all of these, though they won divine approval by [means of] their faith, did not receive the fulfillment of what was promised." [5]

Dr. Vance Havner, in his book *But God,* refers to those who are listed in the Bible's *Who's Who of Faith* as the *"if nots,"* the unshakable in faith who could face the furnace and say, "Our God is able to deliver us—BUT IF NOT . . ." He goes on to say, "God may grant you fame and prosperity or a furnace and obscurity. But be prepared for Faith's Alternative. Whether you stop the mouth of a lion or the lion's mouth stops you, whichever procession you march in, let that be incidental." [6]

Don't think though that God's exceptions are excuses or loopholes! The criterion that will never let you use these examples, or any other, as an excuse is this statement: "They won divine approval by means of their faith." If you know that the condition you are in has God's approval, then you also need nothing more.

Perhaps you've been defeated in the valley of affliction because you've been trying to prove your faith to men. And so when you are not healed, you feel frustrated, deprived of self-confidence. Or perhaps you've been made to feel guilty because you are sick.

I have a friend who will no longer open a book on the subject of divine healing. Afflicted with a chronic ailment, she says that so much of what she read and heard men say to prove their doctrines of healing did nothing but cause confusion, depression, and spiritual defeat.

Confusion often does result because each man stresses that which has been made important to him. It may or may not be God's emphasis to you. Be open to hear and free to receive, but get through to God to know His Word to you, for yourself.

While the ministry of the Spirit does convict, it always is superimposed with hope and the incitement to release faith in the Person of Jesus Christ. The Word of faith for healing may come to you through a man, but it will not be man's opinions, but the Living Word of the Risen Savior which will become life to you.

Because I have come under His rule, I know, "The Lord will perfect that which concerneth me," [7] including that which pertains to my physical body, because when I am committed to the Lordship of Christ, spirit, soul, and body are under His authority. Therefore, physical healing—the time, the place, the means—all that it involves, is under His control. However, this does not necessarily mean "perfect" health. But it does mean He will do all that is needed in my body that I may glorify the Risen Christ.

With Calvary and the empty tomb behind Him, Jesus offers me His Life and His faith. Moment by moment I must draw from the Source to meet my needs. Thus I can walk in victory through the valley of affliction.

Jesus is Lord! And "the Lord is the strength of my life!" [8]

"And whether we be afflicted, it is for your consolation and salvation . . . as ye are partakers of the sufferings, so shall ye be also of the consolation.

"Jesus Christ himself being the chief corner stone; In whom all the building fitly framed together groweth unto an holy temple in the Lord; In whom ye also are builded together for an habitation of God through the Spirit.

"For this cause I Paul, the prisoner of Jesus Christ for you . . ." [1]

—*Paul*

18.

The Ministry of Suffering—in the Valley

There is a dynamic dimension of suffering which few people understand. Think of those who have touched your life with the greatest force. Has it not often been someone who has known much heartache or affliction? But do you know *why* biblically this is so?

I began the journey to discovering why, when I came to know Pastor Foley.

He was a big man, tall of frame, and when he reached out his long arms in leading a hymn it seemed he would embrace the whole audience. Illness had ravished his body until it appeared that only skin held his bones together. But in spite of the physical shackles, the Rev. William J. Foley was a man reckless in spirit.

Whenever he felt the call was of God, it mattered not that he had neither the physical strength nor the stamina for the journey, much less to minister through a series of meetings.

As he called his people to pray, it seemed as though he was crying out with the prophet Jeremiah, "The Word of God is in my heart as a burning fire shut up in my bones, and I was weary with forbearing, and I could not stay." [2]

I had the privilege of working with him to prepare for publication a little booklet which he entitled *Do You Read or Hear God's Word?* Many had tried to persuade him to submit for publication sermon material that had blessed his audiences, but he had his own personal reasons for not doing so. However, during his last weeks with us, he became increasingly perturbed about those who read God's Word without hearing God speak, and without responding in total obedience.

He was flat on his back now, and to write seemed all but impossible. Still he felt compelled to communicate what he believed to be the key to the life of victory. So he began by putting on tape these truths God had made so real to him. A missionary friend transcribed them and prepared the first typed manuscript from which we could work.

Then began the rewriting. There were repeated sessions when Mrs. Foley and I sat at his bedside; she would read a paragraph at a time. Sometimes he would stop her with a shake of head and remark, "That isn't exactly what I want to say."

At last, he seemed satisfied, and since I was painfully aware that time was fast running out, I retyped and prepared the manuscript for mailing. I took it with me to the parsonage on Thursday evening. Someone would be coming later to stay with them through the night. Knowing that Pastor Foley had wanted to enclose a letter to his friend, and editor, Dr. A. W. Tozer, I offered to type it for him while I was there.

As we sat in his bedroom that evening, our hearts nearly broke at his suffering. Even the sound of our voices seemed to cause him pain. When it was time to leave and I bent to tell him good-bye, he asked where the manuscript was. I told him that it was in the other room with the letter to Dr. Tozer and that Mrs. Foley was going to add a little personal note and would mail it in the morning.

"Bring it here, please," he whispered.

I put the pages in his hand. He read only a few paragraphs before they dropped to the bed. Mrs. Foley picked them up and read on. After she had finished, he laid aside his oxygen mask to gasp out in whispers three changes to be made. One was a change in punctuation, the other a couple of words to be inserted, and he wanted to reverse the order of two words! Minor changes, it might seem, but not minor to this man who had fought so valiantly to cling to life for the single purpose of perfecting this work.

Less than forty-eight hours later, he spoke his last word before lapsing into unconsciousness. The word was, *"Pray!"* Early the next morning, at the dawn of the Sabbath, his spirit took its flight, the spirit of a man who had lived recklessly for God, even to his last breath.[3]

"Why?" the people asked themselves and each other. The church had fasted and prayed and thought to believe for their pastor's healing. It was hard to understand why God had taken him from them, but even more difficult to understand why there had first been those long pain-racked months of suffering.

God had given him an answer though, which he shared with me a few weeks before his death. It wasn't an answer that left nothing more to be said, but as a true shepherd of the flock, he accepted it out of love for God and for those God entrusted to him. And I think that he hoped my knowing would cause me to understand something of the dealings of God through suffering. Only recently though, am I beginning to comprehend in any measure this aspect of God's purpose in the valley of human experience.

Something had been happening to the church, and we were talking out our concern. Though he had been spared many of the problems, being sensitive to the Spirit and to the needs of his people, he understood much without knowing details. The church God had given him life to build when he had been brought home from the mission field to die, the church he gave his very life to build, was as close to him as his heartbeat. And now that of which Paul warned

Timothy seemed to be happening. "For the time will come when they will not endure sound doctrine. . . . And they shall turn away their ears from the truth . . ."

His eyes caught mine and held them as he raised one hand to point down at himself.

"Do you want to know why—this?"

It is a moment suspended in memory. And though I think that I already knew, I flinched when I heard him say, "It is for the church!" He was looking to see if I understood what it was he was saying, and then his breath went from him in a gasp and his hand dropped heavily.

"Greater love hath no man . . ." [4] The words spoke themselves. I swallowed hard.

Accepting the valleys for what God would work in us through them, is one thing; accepting them for what He would work in His church is something else. Paul had moved into this sphere of Kingdom living when he wrote, "[Even] now I rejoice in the midst of my sufferings on your behalf. And in my own person I am making up whatever is still lacking and remains to be completed [on our part] of Christ's afflictions, for the sake of His body, which is the Church." [5]

This is a rather startling statement. Did Paul mean that even as Christ's suffering was redemptive, so his suffering—and our suffering too—should be redemptive?

Absolutely not, if one limits redemption to what man is redeemed *from*. But most assuredly, yes, when we rightly consider the overall purpose of God in redemption as including what one is redeemed *to*.

Redemption does not stop with justification; spirit, soul, and body must be restored to the perfect creation of God, and there must again be perfect communication between man and God. So our suffering, when it is a part of God's will, can and will be redemptive, simply because God takes it up into the overall purpose of God which is a redemptive purpose.

In I Peter 3:15–17, we see the difference between suffering which is the backlash of sin, and the suffering which follows our commitment to Christ. We see that their end results are different too. If you acknowledge Jesus as Lord, Peter declares, live so any accusations brought against you are not justified; if you are guilty as accused, it will be painful, but beyond that, such suffering is meaningless. However, suffering ensuing from false accusation is not a sterile affair. As you have been brought to God through the suffering of Christ, so will God use your suffering, when it is according to His will and purpose, to bring others into the full purpose of redemption and the establishing of His Kingdom.

God is not the author of suffering, but He has called us into a life in which the principles of the Kingdom which animate us call for suffering and persecution. Paul and Barnabas had been through something. The bruises Paul had from the stoning at Lystra were for real. And so was what God had been doing in him through persecution. In a little while, he was returning to Lystra, Iconium, and Antioch where he had been treated so cruelly, "establishing and strengthening the souls and the hearts of the disciples, urging and warning and encouraging them to stand firm in the faith, and telling them that it is through many hardships and tribulations we must enter the kingdom of God." [6]

If you think the valleys are just to be endured and you moan your way through the painful experiences of life, forget it! You won't be edified, much less the church. It's when there is that deep commitment that cries out for love of Jesus, "Lord, here's my life, help Yourself to all of it and send me the bill," that affliction becomes efficacious. As you begin to know the application of Christ's claims as Lord, you'll know emancipation from self.

Until then, you cannot see the Eternal Purpose of God objectively. That above and beyond—the Body of Christ (the church)—is the definitive focal point of what God is doing. Not an organization, but a people separated unto Himself established in righteousness, in whom He can reveal Himself to them and to the world.

Peter wrote to a church that was scattered, and he said, what you are going through in your area, your brethren are going through where they are, because God has one purpose—to reveal His glory in the church. Suffering would work to establish, strengthen, settle, and make complete the Body of Christ. God is working through affliction, suffering, persecution—the valley experiences—to the end that the whole Body might be crowned with the eternal glory of the revealed Christ.[7]

Paul said, "I will most gladly spend and be utterly spent . . . for your souls." [8] This is the attitude of one who has caught a vision beyond personal blessing.

Paul shows us clearly how our individual identification with Christ in His sufferings serves the church.

Even so, "Let each one of us make it a practice to please . . . his neighbor for his good and for his true welfare, to edify him—that is, to strengthen him and build him up spiritually.

"For Christ (gave no thought to His own interests) to please Himself; but, as it is written, The reproaches and abuses of those who reproached and abused you fell on Me." [9]

"For just as Christ's . . . sufferings fall to our lot [as they overflow upon His disciples, and we share and experience them] abundantly, so through Christ comfort and consolation and encouragement are also [shared and experienced] abundantly by us." [10]

Never forgetting, "it is God Who confirms and makes us steadfast and establishes us (in joint fellowship) with you in Christ, and has consecrated and anointed us—enduing us with the gifts of the Holy Spirit." [11]

Some today are putting great emphasis on the Body ministry among the fellowship of believers. And it is an exciting part of the charismatic dimension. However, most fail to understand that the ministry of the Body most spoken of by Peter and Paul is the strengthening of the Body through the comfort, the joy, the peace, and the faith that is secured through the valleys when the soul stands fast in Christ despite the most crushing difficulties.

When and where are needs met through the operation of the Spirit? When will prophecy—comfort, edification, exhortation—be most meaningful to you? Quite likely when you are in the pit of depression. The ministry of healing? When you are ill. Faith? When you need deliverance or provision.

One who is on the mountaintop does not need lifting up. One who is in the valley does. The valley is where I need my brother most, as the Spirit channels through him the gifts of healing, comfort, deliverance to relieve my distress.

That which I receive through my brother in my hour of desperation and tears must be rendered again to him and to others, for the anointing of the Spirit is for reciprocal ministry among all believers, to build up one another, that the beauty of the Lord our God may be upon His church.

Total identification with Christ cannot exclude suffering; love and submission to Him give it value. But nothing He does is exclusively mine, not even what God does to strengthen and establish me through the valley experiences.

Thus in the Eternal Purposes of God, suffering—when it is according to His will—becomes a medium for the cultivation of the ministries of the Spirit which will not only meet individual need, but strengthen the whole Body.

Peter says, "As every man hath received the gift, even so minister the same one to another . . . that God in all things may be glorified through Jesus Christ." [12]

Even so, we are not to be passive about suffering, but as we yield ourselves to the working of the Spirit, testing and trial will serve the whole Body of Christ, to fulfill His ultimate purpose for His church, that always and in all things, it will be a church triumphant, strong and unshakable.

"If you are suffering according to God's will, keep on doing what is right and trust yourself to the God Who made you, for he will never fail you.

"Be really glad—because these trials will make you partners with Christ in his suffering, and afterwards you will have the wonderful joy of sharing his glory . . ." [1]

—Peter

19.

Rejoicing in Hope—Triumphant in the Valley

Sometimes when we are going through extreme difficulties, we forget who is the King. Satan would have us believe he is in control, that evil is the reigning force. And to hear some folks' testimony, one might think so; the devil is really giving them a horrible time.

People so freely give credit to the devil. They see the devil in every hard place.

Job wasn't giving the devil any satisfaction by acknowledging his doings when he said, "It is the hand of God that hath touched me." [2]

We need to see God! We need to know that whatever touches us is the hand of God! Regardless of how anything seems, God is still God—the Omniscient, Omnipresent, Omnipotent, Eternal Father.

In the pattern of prayer which Jesus gave to His disciples, commonly referred to as the Lord's Prayer, He concludes by affirming the principles of the Kingdom which merge into the Eternal Triangle of the Godhead.

"Thine is the *kingdom,*
and the *power,*
and the *glory* . . . for ever." [3]

Upon this structure, Paul superimposes another triangle,

"For *of him*,
  and *through him*,
    and *to him*, are all things:
      to whom be glory forever." [4]

In order to elucidate how this must be expressed in our life, we may overlay it with yet another triangle, the attitudes we are to maintain toward "all things":

Take all things from Him;
  Do all things through Him;
    Give all things to Him.

This is how it would look in diagram:

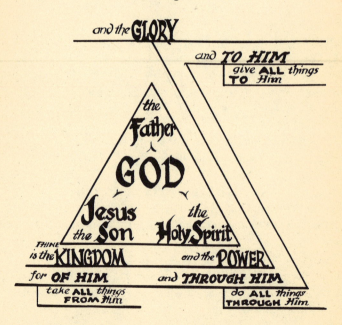

JESUS IS KING . . .

"Thine is the Kingdom . . ." is the word of faith which looks to the past, the present, and the future, and makes one all-embracing commitment to the Self-determined sovereignty of the King. It is our assurance today and our hope for tomorrow. We aren't looking for a King—we have one who is Eternal.

"For *of Him* . . . are all things" recognizes the King as the Source of all things.

It is not unusual for Christians to acknowledge with the lips that "all things are of Him," at the same time having reservations in respect to certain offenses. You need to be thoroughly established in the truth that "all things" do include whatever besets you in the valleys; the trials and afflictions you are going through are all of Him. Regardless—take all things from Him.

Because we are unquestionably in a conflict, it might seem that we often are the victim of the enemy's onslaughts apart from God's doing. While the devil does have certain legal rights determined by God, and he does do battle against the saints, if you have established your security in God, you can accept, without any reservation, all things as being from the Lord. It's amazing how God will take the very thing the devil has thought to use to defeat us, and use it to bring us a greater victory. As a friend puts it so aptly, "The devil is the only one who works for God without pay!"

If you are in Christ, who is in the Father, picture yourself as being encircled by God. The enemy's free territory is limited to outside the circumference of that circle. Absolutely nothing can reach you within that circle which has not first touched the One who gave His life for you. Only willful disobedience can open up a landing strip for the devil. Obedience and faith afford full protection.

On occasion, God does the unusual to confirm His control. So it happened when my husband was injured. The night before the accident, our pastor was out in the shop doing some lettering on one of the trucks. As he told me later, suddenly, the word "explosion" came forcibly to mind. He looked around, wondering if the Lord was alerting him to impending danger. Seeing nothing to cause alarm, he went on with his work. But again the word "explosion" projected loudly into his thinking. Still he found nothing which seemed a potential hazard. Yet, just a few hours later, there *was* an explosion, injuring my husband critically.

He had since been troubled, he said. Was the Lord trying to warn him? Would a greater sensitiveness to the Spirit have prevented Al's being hurt? But even as he was speaking, I knew a great sense of calm, and I told him, "No, I don't think that you missed something God was saying. I'm sure God was just letting us know that He wasn't caught unawares; He knew beforehand; He was in absolute control."

Whenever obedience to Christ demands sacrifice and means persecution, Jesus promises 100 percent interest on such investment in the Kingdom. If you ascribe all trials to the enemy, however, saying the devil has caused your present circumstances, then you are choosing to recognize the wrong Kingdom. What you give the devil credit for taking, God is not obligated to repay; in so doing, you forfeit the "dividends" of the Kingdom.

When we stop merely theorizing about the Kingdom of God, and start accepting the Lord's absolute dominion, seeing all things as being from Him, we will begin to enjoy our legacy. For "the kingdom of God is . . . righteousness, and peace, and joy in the Holy Ghost." [5] It won't make any difference when we walk through the valleys, righteousness, peace, and joy will be our inheritance if the King is reigning.

THE HOLY SPIRIT IS THE PARACLETE (helper, teacher comforter)—The PROMISE OF POWER

"Thine is . . . *the power* . . ." is the acknowledgment of our utter incompetence to achieve on our own any manifestation of His Kingdom. It is recognizing the one and only Source of spiritual energy.

Once we accept that "*through Him* . . . are all things" we will stop dividing our lives into two parts: that which we think we can do on our own, and that for which we consider we need the anointing of the Spirit. Jesus said, "Without me ye can do nothing." [6] And He meant *nothing.* Because anything done apart from Him is nothing more than human effort and thus meaningless.

I think we get trapped here most often by someone asking us to do a certain thing. And for fear of offending we say yes and then struggle through doing whatever it might involve with a sense of futility because we know human effort alone *is* futile.

Surely Scripture teaches that our lives should evidence the power and presence of God. The power of God channeled through the believer by the Holy Spirit does produce signs and wonders, but that isn't what it is all about.

The anointing of the Spirit is not just so that we might live and function in a supernatural realm. It is the power of the Holy Spirit in operation in our lives which enables us to say and do and react pleasing to God in all the little sandpapering affairs of everyday living. Only through the power of God released in our lives are we able to maintain right relationships. Only through the power of God are we able to know the reality of "His Kingdom come on earth" in His manifest will in our lives. Only through the power of God are we able to effectively touch the lives of others.

GOD IS THE ETERNAL FATHER

"Thine is . . . *the glory* . . ." is the kneeling heart worshiping the Father. Not at a moment set apart, but as smoke from an unquenchable flame.

If we take all things from Him, do all things through Him, it will follow: the glory is all His.

In the first chapter of Ephesians, three times Paul stresses that we are called to live "to the praise of His glory." Then he goes on in the letter to establish some very practical guidelines. We cannot hold that our talk, our manners, our demeanor, our personality, our dress are unimportant. The whole man should be directed to glorifying Jesus Christ.

It is God's business to confirm His Word with signs and wonders as He so desires, likewise to reveal His glory. If we have been used when there have been miraculous manifestations of His power, we dare not touch any of the glory. God doesn't demonstrate His power through us to build our kingdom, but His.

It is not only the supernatural that should cause responses that glorify God; the scourging of the spirit should be to the same end. Peter wrote to a suffering church: "But the God of all grace, who hath called us unto his eternal glory by Christ Jesus, after that ye have suffered a while, make you perfect, establish, strengthen, settle you. To him be glory and dominion for ever and ever." [7]

Christ's glory and dominion are inseparable. If we live to the praise of His glory, we will be completely under His dominion. And in living out our commitment to the Lordship of Christ, we will be perfected and established and made strong through adversity.

While we are not to *touch* His glory, the church is the only hope God has of revealing Christ to the world. "Christ in you, the hope of [His] glory." [8] He wants to reveal His glory through us.

This is the Treasure—Jesus within the earthen vessel of our humanity, a vessel broken to reveal the indwelling Christ. In the darkest moments of life, others will be most aware of the light shining forth. And as we ourselves realize God is using persecution, pain, and difficulty for the edification of the church and the glorification of His Son, the darkest valleys will begin to take on an iridescent glow.

The Lord speaking through the prophet Hosea, said: "I will give . . . the valley of Achor for a door of hope." [9]

Why the valley of Achor? Because of the polarity of its past echoes to the triumph of hope.

Here it was that Achan met God's judgment when he took for himself of the spoils of Jericho. No man can hope to conceal buried treasure; it will destroy him. And it had happened here in the valley of Achor; Achan and all that he possessed were stoned and burnt by fire.

Achor represented rebellion, covetousness, defeat, and death. It also represented a people taking desperate measures to rid themselves of everything associated with that sin which had brought them defeat; in so doing, Israel bore witness to being under the absolute authority of God.

Consequently, God declares, that which has known blood and fire shall be a symbol of hope. The valley of Achor which held such tragic memories would be a place of rest where the herds would lie down in green pastures, where the inhabitants would sing for joy. Though Achan, in his greed, had not seen God's provision as sufficient, God's people should know the blessings of a fruitful land, the security of a land at peace, an intimate relationship with the Lord who reigneth over all.

Even so, it is the outpoured Blood of Jesus, and the unquenchable Fire of the Holy Spirit that is our hope, and the hope of all lost humanity. Only through the Blood and the Fire—through the receptivity of faith—do we become the manifest sons of God, anointed, that we may know His blessings and that He may reveal His glory in us.

Trouble came early to Joseph; torn from his family, he had become a displaced person through treachery and treason. However, his acceptance of adversity is remarkable. What a tremendous concept of all his steps being ordered by God, that he could say to his brothers, "It was not you that sent me hither, but God." [10] Furthermore, it was while he was still in Egypt that he declared, "God hath caused me to be fruitful in the land of my affliction." [11]

Even so, it is when we see God in control that the valleys of suffering will become fruitful. We try so hard to avoid the unpleasant, and to a point we should. Certainly we aren't to impose suffering on ourselves. But when we find ourselves in difficult straits, we need to ask, "Lord, what are You trying to say?" Rather than fighting circumstances, we need to accept with thanksgiving the dealings of God through circumstances, being so yielded to His will that He can accomplish all He desires, in and through us.

These are days when the Spirit of God is doing new and exciting things. The Kingdom of God is being built. Our future is not in the hands of the Communists, the reformers, the rebels. Neither does it depend upon circumstances nor our position. Our future is in the hands of the King.

When the shadows are darkest in the valley, be confident. God has never lost one of His children in the valleys yet! The One who is Lord of the hills is Lord of the valleys too! Know "that the trial of your faith, being much more precious than of gold that perisheth, though it be tried with fire, might be found unto praise and honour and glory at the appearing of Jesus Christ." [12]

We have been begotten with a lively hope, wherein we rejoice in the midst of the valleys, looking to that glorious day when Jesus Christ shall be shown forth in the heavens and upon earth to be "the blessed and only Potentate, the King of kings, and Lord of lords." [13]

But until then, I want to be attuned to that which God is doing in this hour; I want to know His purpose in affliction and adversity; I want to know what God wants to communicate through me when I am broken.

As I walk through the valleys, I want everything that I am to bear witness that I have crowned Jesus, Lord of my life. I don't want to create an illusion. I want reality, that He will build His Kingdom within; that He will establish me in Zion, and that I might know the thrill of meeting human need through personal venture.

Notes

Unless otherwise indicated, all Scriptures are taken from the King James Version of the Bible.

Chapter 1

1. Jer. 2:23 (RSV)
2. Ps. 27:1
3. "Face the Inevitable," *Fellowship*, January 1958.
4. Phil. 3:12

Chapter 2

1. Ps. 94:12,13 (*Amplified Bible*)
2. I Kings 20:23
3. I Kings 20:27
4. I Kings 18
5. I John 3:8
6. I Kings 18:41–46
7. Ps. 103:14 (RSV)
8. I Kings 19:8
9. I Kings 19:18
10. Matt. 16:16–17
11. Acts 2:14
12. Acts 2:21
13. Matt. 14:30
14. John 10:10
15. John 16:31 (RSV)
16. John 18:36
17. John 5:25
18. Jude 24, 25 (*Living Bible*)

Chapter 3

1. Isa. 40:27,28; 41:13,18 (RSV)
2. John 16:15
3. Ps. 121: 1,2
4. I Thess. 5:17
5. Matt. 11:15
6. Luke 16:13
7. Job 37:13
8. Ps. 51:10
9. Ps. 51:17
10. John 19:11
11. Isa. 40:1
12. Phil. 3:10
13. Matt. 17:21
14. I Pet. 2:15
15. John 14:28
16. "Triumphant Testimony," *Fellowship*, April-June 1965.
17. Ps. 42:8
18. Phil. 2:13
19. Amos 3:7 (RSV)

Chapter 4

1. Rom. 6:22 (*Living Bible*)
2. II Tim. 2:24,25
3. Luke 17:21
4. Matt. 4:17
5. Isa. 29:13
6. Matt. 15:8,9
7. Mark 7:6,7
8. I Chron. 29:5,9,14
9. Num. 14:24
10. Rom. 6:16

11. Matt. 7:23
12. Matt. 7:21
13. Isa. 42:1
14. I Thess. 5:18
15. Ps. 25:10
16. Exod. 21:5
17. Matt. 11:29
18. Phil. 2:5
19. John 12:26
20. Matt. 6:24
21. II Sam. 15:21
22. John 15:20
23. Ps. 119:71
24. Matt. 6:25
25. Mark 8:35
26. Eph. 1:12
27. John 12:26
28. John 13:15,16

Chapter 5

1. Prov. 17:9 (*Amplified Bible*)
2. Matt. 5:44
3. *Ibid.*
4. *Ibid.*
5. I Cor. 13:4–7 (*Amplified Bible*)
6. Matt. 22:40 (*Living Bible*)
7. John 13:34
8. John 13:1
9. John 17:23,26
10. Col. 1:27
11. Rom. 5:5
12. Eph. 2:4,5
13. Matt. 5:46
14. Matt. 19:16
15. Mark 10:21
16. Phil. 2:3,5
17. I John 4:18
18. John 11:3,5

Chapter 6

1. Ps. 52:1
2. Ps. 42:3 (*Amplified Bible*)
3. I Thess. 5:18
4. Gen. 1

5. Rom. 8:28,29
6. Watchman Nee, *The Release of the Spirit* (Cloverdale, Indiana: Ministry of Life, for Sure Foundation, 1965)

Chapter 7

1. Lam. 3:7
2. Exod. 3:14
3. Exod. 16:3
4. Exod. 16:8
5. Eph. 4:1
6. Acts 9:6
7. Acts 9:16
8. Acts 7:60
9. Gen. 39:21,23
10. Gen. 45:5,8
11. Dan. 6:10
12. Jer. 20:8,9
13. Lam. 3:7
14. Ps. 18:32
15. Ps. 57:7
16. Ps. 32:10

Chapter 8

1. Phil. 1:21–23 (*Amplified Bible*)
2. Ps. 56
3. Phil. 1:22 (*Amplified Bible*)
4. I Thess. 5:18 (*Amplified Bible*)
5. II Cor. 1:8–11
6. John 16:14

Chapter 9

1. Ps. 3:5
2. Ps. 56:3

Chapter 10

1. Jer. 15:17 (*Amplified Bible*)
2. Luke 12:32
3. Matt. 26:39
4. John 16:32
5. Matt. 26:39

6. "Rock of Ages," by Augustus M. Toplady.
7. "The Solid Rock," by Edward Mote.

CHAPTER 11

1. II Cor. 12:5 (*Living Bible*)
2. II Cor. 12:9
3. "He Giveth More," by Annie Johnson Flint.
4. I Cor. 1:5,7
5. I Sam. 17:47
6. II Cor. 10:4,5 (*Amplified Bible*)
7. II Cor. 3:4,5

CHAPTER 12

1. Eph. 3:18,19 (*Living Bible*)
2. Job 9:20
3. Matt. 5:11
4. Ezek. 3:14
5. Ezek. 3:15
6. II Cor. 5:14,16
7. II Cor. 1:3,4
8. Ps. 44:21
9. Prov. 15:8
10. II Tim. 2:19
11. John 14:9
12. Luke 8:2,3
13. Mark 14:8
14. Mark 14:9

CHAPTER 13

1. Isa. 51:14–16
2. I Cor. 1:29
3. I Cor. 15:57
4. John 7:37
5. Luke 11:9–13

CHAPTER 14

1. Jude 20 (*Living Bible*)
2. II Tim. 1:7 (*Amplified Bible*)
3. Phil. 4:6
4. Isa. 30:15

5. Ps. 46:10
6. I Sam. 12:7
7. Jon. 2:7,9
8. Isa. 30:15
9. Heb. 13:15
10. Isa. 9:7
11. Ps. 46:4,5

CHAPTER 15

1. Exod. 14:13,14
2. *Ibid.*
3. II Cor. 10:4,5 (*Amplified Bible*)
4. II Chron. 20:15,17
5. II Chron. 20:12 (author's paraphrase)
6. II Chron. 20:21
7. Rom. 8:38,39
8. John 16:33 (*Amplified Bible*)
9. Rom. 5:2
10. Acts 27:25
11. II Cor. 1:20

CHAPTER 16

1. Matt. 15:6,7 (*Amplified Bible*)
2. Gal. 2:20
3. II Cor. 13:4
4. Jer. 31:3,4,28

CHAPTER 17

1. Rom. 14:7,8 (*Living Bible*)
2. "A Day of Miracles," *Light and Life Evangel*, February 23, 1958.
3. Phil. 1:6 (*Amplified Bible*)
4. Isa. 55:9
5. Heb. 11:38,39 (*Amplified Bible*)
6. *But God*, by Vance Havner (Los Angeles, Calif.: Bible Institute of Los Angeles)
7. Ps. 138:8
8. Ps. 27:1

CHAPTER 18

1. II Cor. 1:6,7; Eph. 2:20–22; 3:1
2. Jer. 20:9 (author's paraphrase)
3. "The Reckless in Spirit," *The War Cry*, November 25, 1967.
4. John 15:13
5. Col. 1:24 (*Amplified Bible*)
6. Acts 14:22 (*Amplified Bible*)
7. I Pet. 5:1,9,10
8. II Cor. 12:15 (*Amplified Bible*)
9. Rom. 15:2,3 (*Amplified Bible*)
10. II Cor. 1:5 (*Amplified Bible*)
11. II Cor. 1:21 (*Amplified Bible*)
12. I Pet. 4:10,11

CHAPTER 19

1. I Pet. 4:19,13 (*Living Bible*)
2. Job 19:21 (author's paraphrase)
3. Matt. 6:13
4. Rom. 11:36
5. Rom. 14:17
6. John 15:5
7. I Pet. 5:10,11
8. Col. 1:27
9. Hos. 2:15
10. Gen. 45:8
11. Gen. 41:52
12. I Pet. 1:7
13. I Tim. 6:15

For a free copy of

LOGOS JOURNAL

send your name and address to

Logos Journal

Box 191

Plainfield, New Jersey 07060

and say, "one free Journal, please."